WE
DID
THAT?

WE DID THAT?

Human Bloopers, Secret Histories, Medical Mysteries, Strange Superstitions, and Other Curiosities from Our Past

SOPHIE STIRLING

CORAL GABLES

Cover Design: Elina Diaz
Cover Photo/illustration: Nattle/shutterstock.com
Layout & Design: Elina Diaz

For permission requests, please contact the publisher at:
Mango Publishing Group
2850 S Douglas Road, 2nd Floor
Coral Gables, FL 33134 USA
info@mango.bz

For special orders, quantity sales, course adoptions and corporate sales, please email the publisher at sales@mango.bz. For trade and wholesale sales, please contact Ingram Publisher Services at customer.service@ingramcontent.com or +1.800.509.4887.

We Did That?: Human Bloopers, Secret Histories, Medical Mysteries, Strange Superstitions, and Other Curiosities from Our Past

Library of Congress Cataloging-in-Publication number: 2020933475
ISBN: (print) 978-1-64250-201-5, (ebook) 978-1-64250-202-2
BISAC category code HUM000000—HUMOR / General

Printed in the United States of America

For Antonio Frexes

"*Never let formal education get in the way of your learning.*"

—Mark Twain

Table of Contents

Introduction: A Cabinet of Curious History 11

We Did That? Bloopers, Blunders, and the Bizarre 13

We Believed That? Superstitions 76

We Prescribed That? Medical Cures, Quacks, and Craziness 114

We Invented That? Surprising and Wacky Inventions 151

We Did That? Pain and Death is Beauty 172

We Did That? Odd Jobs 207

Closing the Creaky Cabinet 228

References 230

About the Author 252

Introduction

A CABINET OF CURIOUS HISTORY

Human history. So much can be imagined from those two simple words: The fall of empires, rising of new nations, founding of new religions, wars, inventions, scientific breakthroughs, mysteries, victories. There is no doubt our species has interesting stories to tell.

Many tales are the stuff of legends, showcasing the beauty, wisdom, and ingenuity of humanity. But other moments from history are full of blunders, weirdness, and endearing foolishness. These are the moments history nerds like me live for. So, instead of blissfully going about our lives feeling proud of our species, I say we take a tour of the cringe-worthy and delightfully embarrassing moments of history to shake things up.

Some might say ignorance is bliss, but I say ignorance is boredom. In your hands you hold a book of unabashed weirdness. We're weird and proud here. So let's entertain ourselves. After all, if aliens are really watching from space, I think we've give them some pretty great reality TV. It's time for us to turn on the channel too!

Let's now amuse ourselves with some of the oddest and funniest moments that we have on record. There are a lot—and I definitely can't capture all our history's greatness and shamelessness in one book. But for a little while, let's take a peek at just one shelf in the cabinet of our curious history.

Sit back, relax, and try not to cringe.

Oh and fair warning: there are puns running amok throughout the pages of this book. The dad jokes have broken loose from their little cages, and I've done nothing to constrain them. In fact, I was drinking a piña colada and working on my tan as I watched them make their prison break. Enjoy.

We Did That?

BLOOPERS, BLUNDERS, AND THE BIZARRE

"The difference between fiction and reality is that fiction has to make sense."

—Tom Clancy

Our Peculiar History

On a daily basis I am amazed. I watch the news, read articles, scroll on my socials…and I observe. Sometimes, I can't believe the crazy stuff I hear. I'm sure you do, too. Did Florida Man really assault someone with a fried chicken drumstick? Did the president really say that? Someone seriously set a world record for the stuffing the most toothpicks in a beard? (Over two thousand toothpicks, by the way.)

Humans are as brilliant as they are barking mad. You can't keep up with us. I can't even keep up with myself sometimes, I admit. But don't judge…I'm pretty sure we've all been on both sides of the "seriously?" fence. We all make our fair share of embarrassing decisions, while at the same time laughing at others' misfortune. History is chock full of these moments, and will continue to be, I'm pretty sure, until we are extinct. Which, if you watch the news, shouldn't be long now!

Bloopity Bloopers

Gatekeeper Out Fishing

Constantinople, now Istanbul, was prime real estate during the Middle Ages. Not only was it the gateway between Europe and Asia, but it was also beautiful, culturally rich, and sat on a busy harbor. It also came with a washer and dryer. Every empire wanted a piece of it. But with two rings of strong walls fortressing the city, it held off over twenty sieges. It was unattainable.

But then, you know how it goes—you want what you can't have. And Sultan Mehmed II of the Ottoman Empire wanted Constantinople badly. So in 1453, he led a siege against the city, without high hopes of succeeding. That was…until one of his men discovered a gate had been left unlocked. The gate, called the Kerkoporta, allowed the invading army to flood through the city, surprising all those inside, and they conquered it with very little resistance. What exactly happened to the gatekeeper? Did he fall asleep at the wheel? Go out fishing in that beautiful harbor with a view? Simply have a bad case of brain farts? We may never know. But I'm sure he probably ended up getting sacked—just like the city. Hehe.

A Jarring Accident

When the great American poet Walt Whitman passed away in 1892, his brain was donated to the University of Pennsylvania. As one of the most prolific writers and brilliant minds in American history, it was a great privilege to have his actual brain in their possession. Can you imagine? I'm sure the veins in his brain rearranged themselves into poems over time.

Anyway, Whitman, who often wrote about phrenology, donated his brain to science. But one day, a young lab technician reported that he'd dropped the jar it was held in, and damaged the brain. Not even the pieces could be saved. *He dropped the poemy brain.*

This was the official story from Dr. Henry Cattell, the head pathologist at the university. But what *really* happened, Cattell took to the grave. The truth is, *he* accidentally destroyed the brain. After he finished making observations for the day, he accidentally forgot to seal the brain, and left it sitting out in the open overnight. By morning, it had completely decayed. Out of fear of what would happen to his career, he kept mum, only torturously confessing the truth in his diary:

> "I am a fool, a damnable fool, with no conscious memory, or fitness for any learned position. I left Walt Whitman's brain spoil by not having the jar properly covered. Discovered it in the morning. This ruins me…"

Poor Dr. Cattell needn't have been so hard on himself for letting Whitman's brain decay. After all, Whitman knew that all flesh was only passing. In his poem "Time to Come," Whitman wrote:

> This curious frame of human mould,
> Where unrequited cravings play,
> This brain, and heart, and wondrous form
> Must all alike decay.

You see? Cheer up, old Cattell.

Thirteen Times a Charm

The Dutch painting, *Het Lam Gods*, translated to "Lamb of God," is the most stolen work of art in history. This 1432 religious oil painting depicts most of Christian mysticism, from the Annunciation (an angel announcing to Mary she would conceive the savior) to the sacrifice of Jesus Christ, symbolized as a lamb, bleeding into a goblet. Painted on oak panel and weighing two tons, this fourteen-by-eleven-foot artwork has been stolen *thirteen* times. That's basically like stealing a very flat, wide, wooden car.

It's a very desirable work of art, not only for its skilled artistry and for its age, but also for its beauty and religious connection. It has been burned, blow up, thrown around, had some panels separated, yet, the bulk of it survives. Eleventh-twelfths to be precise. Its long and twisted history is filled with heists, wars, ransom notes, conspiracy theories, and more.

It was originally created for St. Bavo's Cathedral in Ghent (modern day Belgium), and after its journey around the world, it resides there today. Napoleon was the first to steal it, and since then, it has been stolen by Calvinists, Nazis, Germans, and a host of unknowns. The theft of the last remaining missing panel, "The Just Judges," which belongs on the bottom left corner, is still considered an open case with the Ghent police. So not only is it the most stolen painting in history, but it's also got the longest-running open case, too. The last tip that the police received said that it was hiding in plain sight. So, who knows…next time you're abroad in Europe, keep your eyes peeled.

The *Het Lam Gods* with all its panels intact.

Stormy Weather

King George VI of England was not expected to inherit the throne of Great Britain. He'd always lived in the shadow of his elder brother, Edward, who had been coronated king, but abdicated the throne for love. When this happened, George had to step up. Maybe growing up under the impression that he could take a back seat led to a major gap in George's artistic education.

John Piper was an English painter who specialized in dark, stormy landscapes. He grew particularly popular for his work depicting WWI, but his most striking works were his landscapes. When King George was shown some of Piper's work at an exhibit, he commented to Piper: "Pity you had such bloody awful weather." Oh, Georgie.

Fake News

There are surprising number of embarrassing moments in newspaper history. Before telephones and the internet, it was the source from which our species hoped to gain its trusted news of the world. But the figures behind the ink are human like us, after all. Here are some carved-in-ink headlines to look and smile and/or cringe upon.

"Titanic Sinking. No Lives Lost."

April 15, 1912 became a heartbreaking and chaotic day for the world when the *Titanic* sank into the freezing, dark water of the Atlantic, killing over half of the passengers and crew on board. But the world didn't know that yet. Especially not the *Vancouver World*.

On that fateful Monday, when word first came in about the disaster, the Canadian newspaper rushed to print with the headline "Titanic Sinking. No Lives Lost." Unfortunately, as we now know, they couldn't have been more wrong. Despite the embarrassment, however, it's not all their fault. The wire they received reported that a ship was being towed to Halifax, and that the passengers were OK—it just wasn't referring to the *Titanic*. The *Vancouver World* wasn't alone—several other newspapers mistakenly reported a lack of fatalities or guessed an incorrect number.

Until the dust settles, accurate information can be hard to come by when tragedy strikes. But since it's the business of newspapers to give their readers information as quickly as possible, there have been many editors who counted their chickens before they hatched, so to speak. Inaccurate reporting is not rare, especially in the haze of confusion that accompanies an event like this. The *Titanic*'s demise is one that went down in history, just like this headline, though for very different reasons.

The Wizard of Mars

While many aspects of our galaxy remain a mystery, over the last hundred years, our knowledge about Mars has grown vastly. Take this example: In the early 1900s, it was quite commonplace to believe there was life on Mars, based on the knowledge available. Actual Martians. This article alone from the *Salt Lake Tribune* has a lot of interesting information to enlighten us with.

In 1877, the Italian astronomer Giovanni Schiaparelli reported to have found what he believed were long, thin lines on the surface of the orange planet. He called them *canali*, meaning "channels" in Italian. Many years later, in the late eighteen - early nineteen hundreds, the renowned astronomer Percival Lowell picked up this observation and ran with it.

Lowell hypothesized that the long channels on the planetary surface were the result of Martian engineering—that the inhabitants of the red planet had built an extensive irrigation canal network to draw water from the planet's snowy icecaps in an attempt to save their drying-out planet.

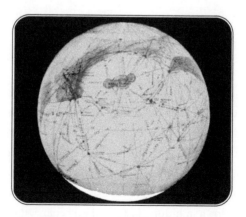

The lines on Mars as drawn by Lowell's team.

Since the appearance of the canals on the planet comes and goes throughout the year, instead of reporting the laughable theory that the Martians were digging them and filling them in yearly, the *Tribune* reported on the theory that the lines we see waxing and waning were formed by *vegetation* lining the banks of the canals. Not the canals themselves.

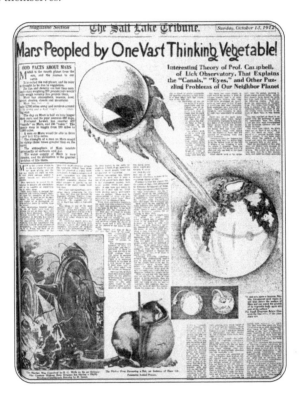

And—in comparing Martian vegetation to earth's carnivorous plants that learn and grow, some began to wonder—why couldn't the plants on Mars evolve intelligently, too? Here's where it gets good!

The *Tribune* further surmised that the vegetation had a mission of its own to keep the planet alive, that there must be a grander intelligence behind the whole scheme: a giant eyeball that sprouted up from the planet's surface:

> "The white spot which we sometimes see [on Mars] is not really a pile of snow but an 'eye'. Supported on a tenuous flexible column, it can raise itself miles above the surface of the planet and watch the operations of its vegetable body at any point."

That so many scientists and astronomers missed this eye isn't surprising, they reassured their readers. The canals had only been seen by a few experts, and many denied their existence at all. They couldn't possibly reach such a theory without this knowledge.

Kind of like the Wizard of Oz, the eye watched over all its vegetable munchkins, and ensured that the planet received its nutrients. But the best was yet to come... Apparently, when this eye was not busy keeping tabs on its planet, it was busy keeping tabs on *us*.

The *Tribune* reports: "When not engaged in watching the physical condition of its body, the great 'eye' makes observations of the earth, sun, planets, stars, and the whole universe. From its vast [position] it is able to see more and farther than all the telescopes of our earth put together." It could be watching us *right now*...

Just to keep with the eerie space theme, here is an aerial photo taken by NASA in 1976, showing a geological formation on Mars that kinda looks like a creepy masked face. Perhaps this is the true face of the Wizard of Mars? Or maybe just another reason to keep you up at night. You're welcome, earthling!

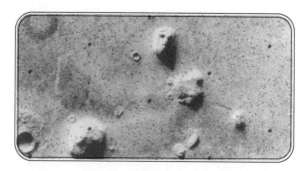

The New Dinosaurs

I'm thankful we can count this section under the category of false predictions. In April 1905, the *Saint Paul Globe* forecasted the downfall of a big chunk of the animal kingdom. The name of the article really says it all. The story begins by describing scientists at the American Natural History Museum fitting together the bones of a brontosaurus—a dinosaur that I think looks like Nessie with four feet. It then predicts how it won't be long "before the bones of animals and birds now familiar to men will be sought, almost, if not quite as eagerly, as curiosities for museums."

The article goes on to list a series of species that have become extinct (that are in reality *not*) such as the bison, sea cow (manatee), and sea lion. Soon to follow the brontosaurus to the grave, they predict, are the musk ox, sea otter, elephant seal, Galápagos tortoise, giraffe, and fur seal. I'll admit, like many scientists, panic is a natural reaction— many species are quickly disappearing from our modern world. But thankfully, most of their predictions have not come to pass yet.

Today, over a hundred years later, the only one of these species that is endangered (but not extinct!) is the Galápagos tortoise. Sea otters are listed as threatened. As luck would have it, the only thing in this case that became extinct is the *Saint Paul Globe*—this edition was one of its very last printings!

The Great Parade of Wild Animals Going to Join the Extinct Brontosaur

Epic Typos

The Missing Hyphen

The space race of the 1950s and '60s resulted in brilliant accomplishments. From sending the first man into orbit, to putting a man on the moon. But, since the work *was* actual rocket science, you can bet there were many flops and screw ups. One particularly epic failure was the infamous mission of the probe Mariner 1 in July of 1962.

Mariner 1 was on a mission to travel to Venus to collect scientific data. But on launch day, only a few minutes after a brilliant liftoff, the internal guidance system started glitching. It began navigating back to earth on a collision course. As it rocketed back towards land, the launch controllers had to hit destruct. Poof! went an 80-million-dollar probe.

What could have gone so wrong? The story goes that in NASA's haste to launch Mariner 1, someone left out one teeny hyphen from the code. One hyphen that sent the rocket off-course. A hyphen that cost millions of dollars, and, of course, a lil bit of Amurican pride.

The Mariner 1, before things went awry.

Shakespyr

As an English major, the foundation upon which my life stands was rocked when I discovered that the spelling of Shakespeare's name isn't specifically confirmed. Many of the historical documents discovered bear different variations of his signature. Perhaps he was lazy. Some hypothesize he didn't know how to spell. After all, his works have noted spelling inconsistencies, like spelling the word "alley" differently (allie, allye) all in the same sentence, and other quirks. During Shakespeare's era, however, spelling was laxer than it is nowadays. Some variations of his name are *Shaksper, Shakspere, Shackspeare*, and *Shakespyr*; the latter being how some of his contemporaries wrote it. Despite the panic I felt upon discovering this fact, I had to tell myself it doesn't truly matter in the grand scheme of things. What's in a name, after all? By another other word his writing would be just as sweet.

Willy's wild signature.

Dord: Insert Definition Here

New words are coined every day. Sometimes by the minute—just watch one of *Saturday Night Live's* "Guy Who Just Bought a Boat" sketches. Or hit up Twitter. People can be so creative.

But in 1934, there was an instance when a word entered the lexicon completely by accident. In that year's *Webster's New International Dictionary* the word *dord* appeared on page 771. How did this super random word get published? Well, you might not know this, because you probably don't read the dictionary on the reg, but the dictionary includes abbreviations for words too. Not just the actual words. (So, for example, in the L section, you could find the abbreviation lb. for pound). The writers were attempting to establish an abbreviation for the word *density*, which, according to the note left for the editors, could be abbreviated with the letters "d or D."

The problem is, this note got placed in the "words" pile instead of the "abbreviations" pile, and the spaces were mistakenly removed from "d or D," giving us the made-up word *dord*. It wasn't discovered until five years later that this word had no instances of usage, nor etymology. Dord was quickly removed from *Webster's New International Dictionary*, but has occasionally appeared in other dictionaries that have a laxer, "Guy Who Just Bought a Boat" approach to wordplay.

Chile Gets a New Name

Typos, as we have seen, can cost money. But they are usually not *on* money. There are only so many words you can fit on a bill or coin. What, like five words max? Still, someone managed to accomplish this against all odds.

In 2008, Chile's national mint manager, Gregorio Iniguez, approved the minting of hundreds of thousands of new coins. They were beautiful. They were shiny. They were perfectly round. But there was one problem…they spelled the country's name wrong. Stamped on these coins was C-H-I-I-E. I'll give them a break. When it's in all-caps, the missing L isn't that noticeable if you're not looking too closely. If you're kind of squinting.

No one noticed the typo until about a year later. The embarrassment was too much for the higher ups, so Iniguez and several others responsible were fired. But hey, the coins are now a collector's item! So if you ever visit this lovely country (where my family is from!) keep your two eyes peeled for two I's.

Why Spinach Means Iron

When you ask yourself how you can get more iron in your diet, I'll bet your mind goes directly to spinach. You aren't alone here! We mostly owe Popeye for this food stereotype, obviously, but there is another reason why "iron = spinach" is so ingrained in our minds.

In an 1870 German study that examined the iron content of spinach, the chemist Erich von Wolf accidentally put the decimal point too far too the right. Instead of reporting that spinach had 3.50 mg of iron, it was instead printed as containing *35.0 mg* of iron—ten times the amount it actually has. As Popeye would say—oh my gorshk!

Unfortunately, the damage was done, and generations grew up with this connection in their minds. Almost sixty years after von Wolf conducted his study, spinach's high iron reputation became even more cemented into our human psyches when Popeye made his 1929 debut. It's still quite the nutritious veggie, make no mistake. But just not *as* nutritious as fame suggests. You'll just have to get Popeye's big guns by other means!

A Case of Mistaken Isledentity

The Island of California

Yes, you read that right. The state of California was once thought to be an island! For over two hundred years, it was depicted on maps as a separate land mass. How did this happen? When Spanish sailor Fortún Jiménez landed on the southern coast of Baja in 1533, he mistook the entire state for an island. If you do a quick search and look at Baja on a map, you'll see that it juts out at the southern tip of the state like a proper peninsula. So his error is understandable. Remember, they didn't have Google Maps back then. Just actual, paper maps. Oh God, you do know what those are, right?

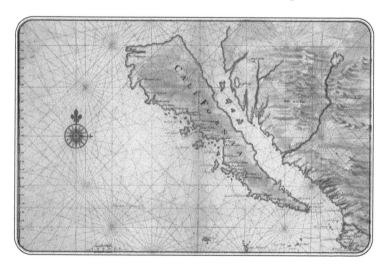

This is, by far, one of the most famous "map errors," and lasted
for over a century! In early 1700s, a Jesuit priest led an expedition
across the Gulf of California, and reported his discoveries, and
his doubts about its "island" status. After more research, by 1747,
King Ferdinand VI of Spain finally decreed that California was *not*
an island.

The Lost Isle of Hy-Brasil

Hy-Brasil, an island known by many names, sits about two hundred
miles off the western coast of Ireland. Or does it? Some say it is
imaginary, and consider it a legend like Atlantis or Avalon. It
supposedly was always shrouded in mists like Avalon, and appeared
only once every seven years.

The name of the island has Celtic origins; the word *Breasal* translates
to "the High king of the world," and the term *breas* translates to
"fortunate," which is why it's also commonly called "Fortunate

Island." But, *unfortunately*, most expeditions that set out to find it never reached the island.

The few who *did* claim to have visited it all had similar experiences. Many claimed it was paradise on earth or "the promised land." Tales of Hy-Brasil describe abundant health, gold-roofed buildings, and rich citizens. Sounds nice! Despite major doubt of its existence, it was even drawn on maps for hundreds of years. It appears as early as 1325, all the way to 1865, when it quite literally falls off the map.

We humans like to solve mysteries, though. Recently, researchers have found submerged landmasses near the rumored location of Hy-Brasil that very well *could* have been islands. So, it's very likely that it was, in fact, a real place! The rising sea levels and geographic shifts in this region are probable culprits for its disappearance.

As you see on the map, Hy Brasil appears right next to the hoof of the animal, as an almost-perfect circle.

Sandy Island Phantom

One of the most recent oops! moments for maps occurred in 2012, when researchers on the academic ship *Southern Surveyor* found only open water where an island was supposed to be. Specifically, Sandy Island. Since the eighteenth century, this island was drawn on maps just off the coast of Australia. But as the researchers approached the place where the island was supposed to be, all they saw was water. It was nowhere to be found.

What happened to Sandy Island? The water reached over a mile deep, so it didn't just get covered by waves. Foregoing the popular Atlantis theory, which is unlikely, given the extensive research of the sea floor, the most likely answer was that it was never there to begin with. There is one theory that French sailors spotted pumice—a light foamy rock that forms after volcanic eruptions—and mistook it for an island. These large rocks can remain the water for years, hence the repeated mapping of this nonexistent island. But it's not exactly the sexiest theory…so, if you're like me, you can just keep on creating more exciting possibilities in your head.

Tax Money Down the Drain

Governments have no shortage of reasons for charging taxpayers—and, apparently, no shortage of bizarre reasons for spending the money either. Here are some fun and creative ways your hardworking wages have been flushed down the toilet with gusto.

☞ Shortly after the bombing of Pearl Harbor, a dentist named Lytle Adams hatched a wild plan. Since bats instinctually dive for cover in buildings when they're out in the open, Adams came up with the idea to fasten actual bombs onto live bats and release them over the targeted territory. A time-delayed fuse would ignite once they were settled in their shelter. He submitted his idea to the US Army Chemical Warfare Service.

They tried it out. In order attach the bombs safely, the bats were forced into hibernation via refrigeration. Not many of them thawed out in time, or when the bats were released the bombs were so heavy they couldn't fly, and just thumped to the ground—a total failure. The cost of this idea: aside from the mistreatment and murder of many bats, 2 million tax dollars.

☞ If you've ever driven on a highway, I'm sure you've felt the slight twinge of nervousness when a large truck encroaches too closely. *Will it be like in the movies, and suddenly tilt on its wheel, and collapse on my car?* What…is that just me? Anyway, The Federal Highway Administration spent $222,000 to study "Motorist Attitudes Toward Large Trucks."

☞ You can now get your dose of culture and history by visiting the Trenton, New Jersey sewer system, which the Environmental Protection Agency spent 1 million dollars preserving as a national monument.

☞ How long does it take you to cook breakfast? Ten to fifteen minutes? Well, the US Department of Agriculture wanted to know for sure. So, they performed a $46,000 study to find out. Answer?: An average of 37 minutes.

☞ The Institute of Museum and Library Services provided a $150,000 grant to The Oregon Museum of Science and Industry, which funded a workshop to determine if gingerbread houses were earthquake-proof. The 2016 workshop was called: "How Does the Cookie Crumble?"

They Failed at That?

If there is one industry fraught with rejection at every angle, it's the book publishing industry. Oh wait. It's the film industry. Oh wait…

Rejection and failure are everywhere. Here are some teeth-gnashing examples of initial failures that eventually led to successes. But, if you are an aspiring author, actor, musician, or artist…rather than feeling dejected, take heart. These instances all show that if you've created a brilliant work of art, if you believe in it and remain determined, you'll succeed. As the popular saying goes, "You can only fail if you stop trying."

Books

George Orwell, *Animal Farm*

This would end up being a double rejection, though the editor from Faber & Faber publishing didn't fully know it at the time. He wrote the following about *Animal Farm*: "We agree that it is a distinguished piece of writing… On the other hand, we have no conviction… that this is the right point of view from which to criticise the political situation at the present time." (Referring to England's alliance with the Soviets.) "I am very sorry, because whoever publishes this, will naturally have the opportunity of publishing your future work: and I have a regard for your work, because it is good writing of fundamental integrity." He was correct. And that "future work" would eventually include *1984*.

JK Rowling, *Harry Potter*

The first *Harry Potter* manuscript was rejected by several literary agents, and at least twelve publishers if not more, before finding its home. When JK was asked about sending out work, she simply replied she always tries to "write better than yesterday."

Dr. Seuss & Co

Theodor Seuss Geisel certainly had imagination. He authored dozens of bestsellers like *The Cat in the Hat* and *Green Eggs and Ham*. Unfortunately, not many editors possessed the same imagination when he first attempted to publish. His first book was rejected by over twenty-five publishers. Since then, his books have collectively sold over 600 million copies.

Film

☞ Before President Ronald Reagan became president, he had a twenty-eight-year acting career. But he was once rejected for an acting role in the 1954 movie called *The Best Man*. Why? Because they claimed he didn't have "the presidential look." I think, eventually, someone thought he did.

☞ A promising young actor auditioned for Universal Studios in 1959, but was rejected. Their reason? "You have a chip in your tooth, your Adams Apple sticks out too far, and you talk too slow." They were referring to Clint Eastwood.

☞ Sidney Poitier was born prematurely, and not expected to survive. His prospects in acting seemed just as slim, even within Black theater circles. When he first auditioned for the American Negro Theater, he was told to get off the stage and go get a job "in a kitchen." To the angered director, Poitier's heavy Caribbean accent was too thick, and he misread his lines. With practice, Poitier worked on his craft, and eventually became the first Black actor win the Academy Award for Best Actor, after being twice nominated. He went on to win numerous Golden Globes and BAFTAs.

Music

☞ U2 was rejected by RSO Records in 1979, the rep saying they were "not suitable for us at present." The next year, they released their first international single "11 O'Clock Tick Tock," and the rest is history!

☞ Ignacy Paderewski, who eventually became Prime Minister of Poland, as well as a talented musician and composer in his own right, was always told his hands were too small to play piano.

Paderewski went on to become one of the greatest concert pianists of all time.

☞ Decca Records rejected the music of a boy band in 1962, saying "guitar groups are on their way out." The band in question? The Beatles.

☞ Enrico Caruso became the most celebrated (and highest paid) Italian opera singer in the early twentieth century, but was always told to forget about opera, because he had a voice that sounded like "wind whistling through a window."

Science

☞ Sir Isaac Newton was initially fated to be a simple farm boy. His mother took him out of school at about the young age of fifteen to work on, and eventually run, their farm. This was a pity, since after an encounter with a school bully, Newton started to excel in school as a way of besting his rival by becoming the star student. Newton fared terribly as a farmer. He was completely disinterested in the work, and failed at it. Finally, his mother put him back in school. He then went on to attend Cambridge University.

☞ Throughout his early life, Charles Darwin was considered an average student. Most of his family were scientists and doctors. His father hoped he would follow in his footsteps, but even the sight of blood made him queasy. His father then suggested he become a parson instead. Luckily for us, Darwin preferred to observe and study nature. This unusual calling fell slightly within the family precedent, as his grandfather was a renowned botanist. Despite being an average student in the classroom, Darwin was a successful student of life. His observations during his travels contributed to *The Origin of the Species*.

☞ From a young age, Thomas Edison was very curious, often self-teaching through reading. However, when he was growing up, his teachers claimed he was "too stupid to learn anything," and he was fired from his first two jobs for not being "productive." He didn't let this stop his curiosity and personal drive, however. There is no way to know if it was his very first invention, but he took out his first patent in 1869 for an electric vote recorder, to speed up the voting process. It unfortunately ended up being a commercial failure, and from then on, Edison vowed only to invent things the public would want. After this, it's was only a few years, and a few patents later that Edison achieved fame for his phonograph invention in 1878. His next challenge: electricity. When a reporter asked him one day how it felt to "fail 1,000 times," on his route to inventing the light bulb, Edison replied, "I didn't fail 1,000 times. The light bulb was an invention with 1,000 steps."

Humans Say the Darndest Things

Trouble with Numbers

"The single most important two things we can do…"
—Tony Blair, former British Prime Minister

"I hope that history will present me with maybe two words. One is peace. The other is human rights."
—President Jimmy Carter, interview in *Philadelphia Daily News*

"I tell you, it's Big Business. If there's one word to describe Atlantic City it's Big Business."
—Donald Trump

"Remember, there's only one taxpayer—you and me."
—John Kushner, Calgary city councilman

Judge: "What inspired you to make this invention?"
Contestant: "Two words: nachos."

"We are trying to change the 1974 constitution, whenever that was signed."
—US Republican Representative Donald Ray Kennard

"Half this game is 90 percent mental."
—Danny Ozark, Philadelphia Phillies manager, regarding baseball

Trouble in General

"So, where's the Cannes Film Festival being held this year?"
—Christina Aguilera

"I'd like to start somewhere small, like London or England."
—Britney Spears, upon being asked if she would ever do a musical

"The Holocaust was an obscene period in our nation's history. I mean in this century's history. But I didn't live in this century."
—Former US Vice President Dan Quayle, 1989–1993

"What is Walmart? Do they sell wall stuff?"
—Paris Hilton, early 2000s, on her reality show *The Sweet Life*

"I definitely want Brooklyn to be christened, but I don't know into what religion."
—David Beckham, talking about his son, Brooklyn

"It's okay to have beliefs, just don't believe in them."
—Guy Ritchie

"I think people think I like to think a lot. And I don't. I do not like to think at all."
—Kanye West

"We're the country that built the Intercontinental Railroad."
—US President Barack Obama, referring to the
Transcontinental Railroad

"I deny the allegations and I deny the alligators!"
—An indicted councilman from Chicago

"A zebra cannot change its spots."
—US Vice President Al Gore

"I don't make predictions. I never have and I never will."
—Tony Blair, former British Prime Minister

"I think that gay marriage is something that should be between a man and a woman."
—Arnold Schwarzenegger, 2003

"I love sports. Whenever I can, I always watch the Detroit Tigers on radio."
—US President General Ford

"These are good times, but only a few know it."
—Henry Ford, in 1931, during the Great Depression

Just Plain Odd

"My heart is as black as yours."
—Mario Procaccino, a former white mayoral candidate for New York, speaking to a Black audience

"Apollinaris, doctor to the emperor Titus, had a good crap here."
—Apollinaris, ancient graffiti found on a wall in Pompeii

"Let the bears devour me."
—Ancient graffiti found near Mount Vesuvius

"Apelles Mus [was here] with his brother Dexter. We had a great time [literally, lovingly], had sex twice—with two girls."
—Ancient graffiti found near Mount Vesuvius

"We peed in the bed, I confess; we have erred, innkeeper. If you ask why, there was no chamber pot."
—Ancient Roman graffiti

"Shakespeare, the great playwright of Arab origin."
—Muammar Gaddafi, eccentric Libyan leader, comparing the playwright's name to Sheikh Zubayr

"You're so concerned with what the public thinks that it gets in the way of what's best for us!"
—Jeanette Smith, a Vesta, California council member—in response to other council members protesting a dinner paid for with public funds

"Speaking of animals, he married his wife, Susanne, when he was in college."
—Mike Leavitt, governor of Utah, when introducing Senator Larry Craig

Verbal Jousting

"One reason the human race has such a low opinion of itself is that it gets so much of its wisdom from writers."
—Wilfrid Sheed, writer

"He is a bad novelist and a fool. The combination usually makes for great popularity in the US."
—Gore Vidal on fellow writer Aleksandr Solzhenitsyn

"I like your opera. I think I will set it to music."
—Ludwig van Beethoven, to another composer

"One man alone can be pretty dumb sometimes, but for real bona fide stupidity there ain't nothing can beat teamwork."
—Mark Twain

"The play was a great success, but the audience was a disaster."
—Oscar Wilde

"You should never say bad things about the dead, you should only say good… Joan Crawford is dead. Good."
—Bette Davis

"I never forget a face, but in your case, I'll make an exception."
—Groucho Marx

"Only two things are infinite—the universe and human stupidity, and I'm not so sure about the former."
—Albert Einstein

We Named It That?

Creativity is one of humanity's greatest gifts. Especially the way we use it in the art of wordplay. Here are some interesting ways we've combined the two!

Quirky City Names

Lemu, Finland

The word *lemu* translates to "bad smell." Don't be put off though, as it's a quaint little town with lovely architecture from the Middle Ages.

Accident, Maryland

This little American town has a miniscule population of around three hundred souls. Someone born there is called "an Accidental." Townspeople with a sense of humor. I like it.

Poo, Spain

A lovely little town with scenic beaches. Luckily a name is not everything.

Normal, Illinois

This city, about a two-hour drive from Chicago is probably, as you would expect, just average.

Oed, Austria

Going along with the normal theme, the name of this beautiful town translates to "boring." It might have a slow social scene, but it sure looks beautiful!

Chicken, Alaska

This mining town left over from the gold rush is almost too small to be called a city. The population has hovered between twenty people and under in the last few censuses.

Cut and Shoot, Texas

One of the odder city names in the state of Texas, with a population of around a thousand.

Embarrass, Minnesota

Aside from its weird name, this town is mainly known for being the coldest in the state of Minnesota.

Llanfairpwllgwyngyllgogerychwyrndrobwllllantysiliogogo-goch, Wales

This town's name takes at least two or three lungfuls of air to pronounce, but most just call it Llanfair. It takes the cake for being the city with the longest name in Europe.

Odd Names of Real People

Crystal Metheney ❧ A Florida woman

Chris P. Bacon

Pid Purdy ❧ American baseball player

Mike Litoris

Sam Sung ❧ A specialist at Apple

Flavour Balls

Muffin Lord

Batman Bin Suparman ❧ A young man from Singapore

Jesus Condom

Dixie Normous

Anurag Dikshit

Matthew Correspondent ❧ A correspondent for BBC News

Wendy Wacko

Filet Minyon

Sue Yoo ❧ A lawyer, if you can believe it!

Brands, Stores, and More

Ash Wipe Chimney Sweeps ☞ A business in Illinois

Ooooh Girl Who Did Your Hair Salon ☞ Get your hair done at this salon in Albuquerque, New Mexico

Curl Up & Dye ☞ Another hair salon with a sense of humor

Wok This Way ☞ A Chinese restaurant in San Francisco

Vinyl Resting Place ☞ You simply *know* this record store is in Portland, Oregon

Let's Get Stoned, Inc. ☞ A business that specializes in kitchen granite countertops and vanities

Planet of the Grapes ☞ A wine bar in London

Surelock Holmes ☞ A locksmith out of Portsmouth

Spruce SpringClean ☞ A witty carpet and upholstery cleaning service in Britain's Cornwall

Animals

Gilbert's potoroo ☞ A sort of rat kangaroo, endangered

Spiny lumpsucker ☞ A teeny fish that sucks on surfaces

Pleasing fungus beetle ☞ I guess it sort of looks like a ladybug

Pink fairy armadillo ☞ Should really be considered a Pokémon come to life

Satanic leaf-tailed gecko ☞ About as cute a gecko as the name suggests

Tasseled wobbegong ☞ Kind of like a shark in the shape of a carpet

Ice cream cone worm ☞ Sometimes we just have to keep it simple

Bubal hartebeest ☜ An extinct antelope-looking creature

Boops boops ☜ A species of seabream fish

Fried egg jellyfish ☜ Actually looks like it sounds!

WHERE DID THAT COME FROM?

Adam's Apple

Like many everyday names, the one Adam's Apple is overlooked. But its origin is simple and quite literal. While, of course, there is no way to know if Adam and Eve indeed ate an accursed apple (or any fruit), the Adam's Apple got its name, because it was believed that Adam got a piece stuck in his throat. It's simply a piece of cartilage (females have it too, though it's less pronounced).

Tying the Knot

This common wedding phrase comes from an ancient Irish Druid tradition called "handfasting," where a Druid priest would tie together the hands of the bride and groom during their ceremony to symbolize their new unity. The tradition still persists today!

Daring Feats

Train Raiders

Józef Piłsudski was a passionate Polish statesman with freedom on his mind. Poland had been split up in the late 1700s, and occupied during a series of invasions from Russia, Prussia, and Austria for many years. On a mission to free his people from occupation, and form an independent Poland, he needed money, and lots of it. On September 26, 1908, mere hours before embarking on a dangerous train robbery, he wrote a letter to his friend as a sort of last will and testament saying, "Money…may the devil take it! I prefer to win it in a fight than to beg for it from the Polish public which has become infantile through being chicken-hearted. I haven't got money and I must have it for the ends I pursue."

He and twenty others, both men and women, gathered in Bezdany, Lithuania for their heist. Their target: a mail train filled with tax money heading to Russia. Six of the robbers were posing as passengers, the rest waited in the wings to strike. As the train rolled in, one group seized power in the station and cut off outside communication. Another group attacked the train itself with bombs and firepower to break through the fortified mail car. The scene was reminiscent of an old film; they stuffed the money into cloth bags—over four million dollars' worth of taxes in today's value. With their loot secured, they separated into different cars, and went off in different directions. Not only was it one of the most successful train robberies in history, but the money kept Piłsudski's secret military organization running for many years. In 1918, Poland officially became an independent country, with Piłsudski as their first leader.

The Last Stand

If you're looking for one Oscar-worthy fight, pitting an underdog against a powerful enemy, look no further than the last stand of Eger in the sixteenth century. The city of Eger was one of the last strongholds of the Ottoman Empire, in Hungary. The Turks were seeking to expand their territories, and Eger was a strategic key. It allowed access to the nearby city of Kassa, which contained silver and gold mines that provided Hungary with wealth, and it also provided a path to Vienna, potentially allowing them to siege that city as well.

About eighty thousand Turks surrounded the city in a historically significant siege. Eger had a mere two thousand souls who vowed to defend their home from invasion, even though they were outnumbered fifty to one. The Turks attacked with more than 150 pieces of artillery and 15 large cannons. They planted bombs under the walls, fired at the walls, sent flaming arrows above the walls—all to no avail. After thirty-nine days, the Turks admitted defeat. The people of Eger had lost about a third of their number, but had somehow still managed to beat back thousands. This siege became an example of heroic patriotism and bravery for Hungary, and the rest of us.

The Boxers That Could

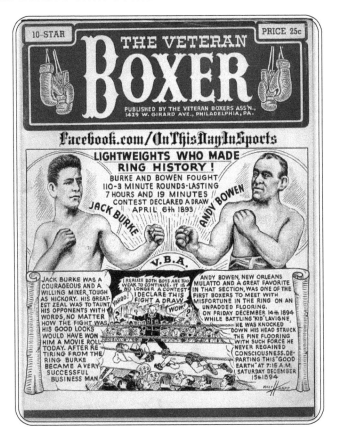

Andy Bowen and Jack Burke could not be kept down. These two boxers fought a match in 1893, in New Orleans, Louisiana that went down as the longest in history. They fought for *seven hours* and nineteen minutes. That's almost a full day at the office. The match was split into rounds that lasted three minutes each…and there were 110 rounds. But get this. At the end of the match…neither of them won. They both kept going, kept fighting, and the referee finally had to call it a draw.

Even though both of Burke's hands were broken, both had sustained several injuries, and each was teetering on the brink of exhaustion—they kept going. The nine thousand fans who showed up had slowly began checking out as the hours passed. The match started at eight in the evening, and it kept going until three in the morning. By the end of the match, they had each lost ten pounds. There were probably that many people in the audience at the end of the match too.

They were fighting for the title of Lightweight Championship of the South, and a grand prize of $2,500, which is about $60,000 in today's money. The referee suggested they split the prize.

This remarkable feat shows the capacity of willpower. They didn't have to box for seven hours—just the next three minutes. And break. And go in again for just three minutes. Their physical stamina and strength is, of course, unbelievable. But what is even more astounding is their mental discipline and daring nerve to not give up.

Oddest World Records

Have you ever wondered how many ketchup packets you could open (without tearing) in thirty seconds? What about how many fortune cookies you could read aloud, and then eat in one minute? Yeah, me too. And so did some ingenious, forward-thinking record breakers. Now, just to wave a disclaimer banner, there are people who pick up the gauntlet, and try to beat these odd records all the time—so please note these are accurate only as of this writing and will surely be beat at some point. Obviously. Who *wouldn't* feel the need to break a brand-new record for the greatest height from which to drop a hot dog wiener directly into a hot dog bun?

- ☞ We might never know how many licks it takes to get to the center of a Tootsie Pop, but Emily Wilson sure knows how much time it takes to lick a candy cane into a sharp point. It took her a measly 2 minutes and 54.84 seconds to get it needle-sharp. Maybe she wanted to stab Santa Claus or something.

☞ The shortest song in the world is "You Suffer" by Napalm Death. It is exactly 1.316 seconds long. Take a listen—it will literally take you less than two seconds.

☞ Thaneshwar Guragai, from Nepal, is a veteran record-breaker. As of this writing he holds fourteen world records, and counting. My personal favorites are the record for spinning a basketball on his toe for the longest duration (20 seconds), and when he spun a basketball on a toothbrush (that he held in his mouth) for the longest duration, exactly 22.41 seconds.

☞ Speaking of toes, here's a feat may be the longest held: there is an ancient Norse sculpture of a man playing the lute with his toes, circa CE 800. He might be the only one known to have strummed the lute in this manner, though there are individuals who can play guitar with their feet.

☞ Scott Reynen is the guy who wore the most hats at once—51 hats to be precise. What did he have to say for himself? "Hats are surprisingly heavy."

☞ The most pairs of underwear worn on a head is 47, by Paige Herbert from California. And in other news about things from "down under," an Australian man named Steve Jacobs takes the record for the most underpants worn (in the "normal" way)—with a circulation-defying 266 undies.

☞ There are many things I don't know in this life, but this is one thing I know for sure: you can definitely get a Coca-Cola at Arby's. The largest advertisement poster ever was 28,922.10 square meters (about half the size of Windsor Castle), and the only thing it said was, I kid you not, "ARBY'S NOW HAS COKE." Message received!

☞ Canadian woman, Mel Sampson, takes the cake (or pizza?) with the record for most slaps of pizza to the face in 15 seconds—210 hot, cheesy slaps.

☞ Another Canadian (what's with you guys?), Craig Morrison, squeezed open the most ketchup packets (without tearing) in thirty seconds—a total of 7 packets. It must've looked like a bloodbath.

☞ The record for the most neck ties worn at once was accomplished by Opus Moreschi with 97 ties. If you dare to take up the gauntlet, it will take both skill (not many people know how to properly assemble *one* tie, let alone ninety-seven), and some strong circulation to beat this guy.

☞ My personal favorite world record is "the most questions asked during a single visit to a drive-thru." Steve Fester asked 33 questions of the poor soul working the window that day. I'm sure you've been to a drive-thru at some point in your life, and know how hard it is to just ask *one* little question. My favorite of the questions he asked is question 23, "Can I get a Big Mac McMuffin?"

☞ Just like throwing the javelin at the Olympics, Josh Fleischer from Florida holds the record for the longest distance to toss a printer. Yes, an office printer. He threw that sucker 26 feet and 6 inches.

☞ California native, Dan Kendall, built the tallest VHS tower at 6 feet 3 inches. Over in Illinois, Brian Pankey holds the record for the longest time to balance twenty-five VHS tapes on his chin. He held it for 7.15 seconds.

☞ Rolly chairs are the best. I don't understand the purpose of stationary ones. I protest their existence! At the very least you can roll from one place to the next, and at the very best you can perform "the longest office chair chain pulled by a motorcycle." The office? Widen and Kennedy's.

☞ The record for the largest "beard" made of Lucky Charms goes to Justin Gignac from New York! His beard was made of 61 charms. You know you tried this when you were younger. The only criteria for this record: the only adhesive allowed is milk, you must use the marshmallows, and all the charms must be placed in the normal beard region. I'd have such a hard time not eating them off my face. To all those trying to beat this record…good *luck*!

WEIRDNESS PERSISTS

We Still Do That?—Drop Cap

You might wonder why the first letter of every chapter sometimes appears in large font, as it does in this book. This is called "drop cap." Using drop cap started in Medieval times when book were not written with any chapter or section breaks (simply continuous writing). So, in order to mark the start of a new section, idea, or train of thought, the scribe would simply use a big, decorative letter. Nowadays, we use clear chapter and section breaks, so drop cap is redundant. But I'm using it in this book for two reasons: First, being ironic is my favorite pastime. Secondly, this is a history book, sometimes covering the Medieval period, and I like to bring things full circle.

Niche Obsessions

Sometimes, obsession turns into mania; sometimes, mania stems from obsession. But, I think the age-old riddle applies: which came first, the chicken or the egg? I couldn't tell you, but I *can* say some of the people mentioned below *are* egg heads.

The Bell Ringer

Crazy runs in the blood, and nowhere is this more apparent than in tales of royalty. One could write several books on all the nutty royals throughout history, and still not document all their weirdness. One such weirdo was Tsar Fyodor I of Russia, who had an inexplicable obsession with bells. He was crowned in 1584, after the passing of his father, Ivan the Terrible (a great act to follow).

Having such a parent as Ivan the Terrible may have had the opposite effect of what his father hoped for, as Fyodor was a passive ruler, mostly concerning himself with piety—which gave him an excuse to visit and ring every church and monastery bell in Russia. His obsessions became so well-known that he was often referred to by two names: Fyodor the Blessed, and Fyodor the Bell Ringer.

President of Skinny-Dipping

John Quincy Adams, the sixth president of the United States, woke at the same time every morning, wrote in his journal, and went for a dip in the nude, without fail. Perhaps, not *fully* nude—he did wear goggles, and a swimming cap. But, even if people were close by, Mr. President would take to the waters in his birthday suit. One might say he was the founder of skinny-dipping.

Once he began this routine, sometime around middle age, he kept up the practice well into his elder years. Despite many dangers and near-death accidents, he simply couldn't deny the great effects on his health. In 1822, Congressman Charles Jared Ingersoll wrote:

> Mr. Adams ascribes his uninterrupted health during the several sickly seasons he has lived in Washington to swimming. He walks a mile to the Potomac for 8 successive mornings from 4 to 7 o'clock, according as the tide serves, and swims from 15 to 40 minutes, then walks home again. For the 6 mornings of low tide he abstains, swimming 8 days out of 14. I have no doubt that it is an excellent system. (He is extremely thin.)

There is a famous story that the reporter Anne Royal once hid the President's clothes until he agreed to do an interview with her. But this (likely anti-feminist) rumor has been debunked as myth. Royal and the president were good friends, so there was no need for her to catch the president in the raw just to hear his thoughts on unemployment rates.

Sugar for the Sultan

Ibrahim I was a Turkish sultan in the 1600s, and was known as one of the quirkiest rulers of the Ottoman Empire. The main reason he even became sultan was because his older brother (who had killed all his *other* younger brothers) left him alive, because he didn't see Ibrahim as a threat; he seemed too mentally disturbed. Instead, Ibrahim was kept in confinement for most of his life, as his brothers were killed off one by one. He had been imprisoned for so long—since he was eight-years-old—that the constant fear of being killed next likely unhinged his delicate mental state even further. But once his older brother died,

Ibrahim was next in line to become sultan. Time to shine, baby brother.

One of the biggest things that made Ibrahim so memorable was his obsession with obese women. It was reported that one time he saw the lady parts of a cow—yes, an actual cow—and became so fixated on them, that he sent out his agents to find the largest ladies in the land, particularly ones who had similar-looking parts. Cringe away.

From the northern part of the Ottoman Empire, one agent returned with a woman weighing about 350 pounds. Apparently, she fit the bill. She became his favorite concubine out of the *three hundred* women he kept in his harem. He was so pleased with her, that he gave her a salary, and the government position of Governor of Damascus. And the best part? He nicknamed her *şeker pare*, literally translated to "little piece of sugar." Doesn't *that* leave a nice taste in your mouth.

Niche Phobias

> *"I have three phobias which, could I mute them, would make my life as slick as a sonnet, but dull as ditch water: I hate to go to bed, I hate to get up, and I hate to be alone."*

—Tallulah Bankhead

Eisoptrophobia

This is not for vain people. This phobia is the excessive fear of mirrors, or, more accurately, seeing yourself in a mirror. It is commonly attributed to a traumatic event in one's life, or superstitious hysteria.

Aritmophobia

All my fellow math-haters will understand this one. Aritmophobia is the fear of numbers. Those who suffer from this condition usually have trouble with their finances, reading traffic signs, or understanding pricing systems in stores.

Ergasiophobia

Anyone with advanced procrastination skills, like me, will vibe with this phobia. Ergasiophobia is the fear of work. It was described by nineteenth-century politician William Upson, in 1905, as "the art of laziness." Some have connected it to long-term job stress, performance anxiety, and fear of failure.

Pteronophobia

This odd word means the fear of feathers, or being tickled by feathers! If you're wondering at the strange etymology, pteron is simply the Greek word for feathers. As with most phobias, it may be caused by a childhood experience, or simply the fear of something happening, i.e. getting sick as a result of the discomfort of being tickled.

Pogonophobia

"Fear the Beard" sounds like it could be the name of a cool reality show following the lives of either a badass biker gang, or a too-cool group of hipsters. But anyway, pogonophobia is the fear of beards.

Bizarre Is a Verb

"The professors must not prevent us from realizing that history is fun, and that the most bizarre things really happen."

—Bertrand Russell

Putting on Airs

In other words, here are some uncommonly known facts, as well as some poems (yes), about farts and their parts.

☞ According to Urban Dictionary, a Mozart fart means "to cut the cheese in a particularly tuneful way." You'll be quite shocked to know this musical mastermind, Mozart, had a certain obsession with flatulence and its cousin, poop. Here is a poem he wrote in a letter to his mother:

> Yesterday, though, we heard the king of farts
> It smelled as sweet as honey tarts
> While it wasn't the strongest of voice
> It still came on as a powerful noise.

He wrote the lyrics to a composition "Leck mir den Arsch," which translates to "Lick my arse." He also penned many letters with snippety lines that are the stuff of legend. Tread lightly if you're easily offended! Some crude clips include: "I now wish you a good night, shit in your bed with all your might, sleep with peace on your mind, and try to kiss your own behind." Or, "*Oui*, by the love of my skin, I shit on your nose, so it runs down your chin." Poetic!

☞ Seventeenth century-poet Sir John Suckling wrote a poem of love, pain, and flatulence that goes like this:

> Love is the fart
> Of every heart:
> It pains a man when 'tis kept close,
> And others doth offend, when 'tis let loose.

☞ Hitler was stricken with uncontrollable farts for many years of his life, often leading to such exquisite pain that he "could scream." I'd say he was already slightly unhinged, but I'm sure constant abdominal cramping and gas didn't help his state of mind. He nearly poisoned himself with the medications his doctors prescribed him, which ranged from strychnine (poison) to atropene (nervous system blocker). While I think his affliction was sort of a divine punishment (though nowhere near what he deserved), some say it was likely caused by his vegetarian diet, which is pretty ironic, if you ask me.

☞ Benjamin Franklin wrote an essay called "Fart Proudly," to the Royal Academy of Brussels, encouraging them to find a way to make farts smell better. After all, if the food we ate affected the way our wind smelled—couldn't that work in the opposite way to a greater advantage? He challenged them to find a chemical or drug to mix in one's food that "shall render the natural discharges of wind from our bodies, not only inoffensive, but agreeable as perfumes." He said this discovery would actually be useful to society—insinuating that many of their studies were, in fact, utterly useless. He closes his letter by stating that the latest study he read was not worth a FART-HING.

☞ Farting as entertainment became such a popular pastime that we needed a name for it. Just as there are comedians, violinists, and artists—well, there are also flatulists, or fartists. Joseph Pujol was a French flatulist in the early twentieth century, famous for being able to control the length and timbre of his wind to imitate people, animals, and melodies. His stage name was "La Pétomane," which roughly translates to "the elastic anus." You're welcome for this information.

Choreomania: The Happy Plague

Also known as "dancing mania" or "St. Vitus's dance," choreomania is a dancing fever that may quite possibly be the most cheerful ancient plague. By the way, St. Vitus was the patron saint of dancing in the Holy Roman Empire. The fever to get jiggy with it swept over crowds of people, from dozens, into the thousands, beginning as early as the seventh century and continuing into the seventeenth. Large groups would take to the streets, and begin dancing erratically, each catching the bug, and they couldn't stop until they passed out from exhaustion. In Strasbourg, France in 1518, it was reported that nearly four hundred people danced nonstop for over a month for no apparent reason. Many theories were thrown around about why this dancing fever happened, from religious fanaticism, to physical illness, and even demonic possession. The Swiss alchemist and astronomer, Paracelsus, however, had his own opinion on the matter:

"Such diseases have nothing to do with the works of the saints... The cause is in the laughing veins which comprehend their spirit in such a subtle way that they are tickled into dancing and joy."

Getting Physical: Sports

The Delicate Art of Shin-Kicking

There is an old sport, popular in England and Wales, called shin-kicking, also known as purring or hacking. It dates to the 1600s, but is still practiced today! Some describe it as an English martial art, where the two opponents grasp each other's shoulders with straight arms, and continually kick the other's shins, trying to knock their opponent to the ground first.

You can only pad your pants with straw, nothing else. It's like an ancient version of "meet me in the parking lot, I'm going to punch you in the face." But instead, it's "meet me in the field," and they're going to kick you in the shins. Whoever can endure the most pain wins. If you've had enough, you can always call out "sufficient," but what self-respecting Englishman would dare admit defeat? Best two out of three.

Cheese Rolling: A Sport for Foodies

This is one competitive sport I can get behind. Cheese rolling is a sport local to Gloucestershire, England, where competitors run after a ball of cheese. It dates to at least 1826, though many locals believe it was practiced earlier. The book *Sports Weird-O-Pedia* noted: "It is not a team sport, but an individual pursuit." I totally agree—my cheese obsession is an individual pursuit that none can understand.

To get the game rolling, large wheels of cheese are taken to the top of a steep hill. Competitors wait at the top as well. Then, the wheel of cheese is set loose to roll down the hill, quickly picking up speed as the humans give chase. The first person to the bottom of the hill wins. What is the grand prize? Guess. It rhymes with sneeze.

The Great Baby Cry-Off

Normally, the goal of new parents is to get their crying babies to put a sock in it. But you'll be tickled to know that every year in Tokyo, a tournament is held where parents enter their babies into a competition against each other to see who can cry the most ferociously. This counterintuitive (and probably headache-inducing) tradition stems from the belief that a crying baby will grow up to become happy, healthy, and prosperous—oh, and it will also ward off demons. The practice is called Naki Sumo. There are many similar beliefs throughout the world, as you'll see in the next chapter on superstitions.

The Naki Sumo name comes from the saying "*naku ko wa sodatsu*" which roughly translates to "crying babies grow fat." As you may be aware, having a rounder shape isn't considered a bad thing in all cultures. Have you *seen* Buddha? He looks pretty blissed out.

At the Naki Sumo Crying Festival, it's baby against baby in a sumo wrestling ring. All entrants must have been born within the year. Upon arrival, parents hand their newborns over to an apprentice sumo wrestler, and they face off against another baby and apprentice. When the battle begins, the apprentice sumo wrestlers hold the babies in their arms, and do all they can to scare them into crying. They make scary faces. They put on scary masks. They yell "Cry! Cry! Cry!" into their little chubby faces. All while a referee judges. What exactly is he judging? The baby that cries first, longest, and loudest of all. The winner's prize? A prosperous, healthy, hopefully rotund life, of course!

We Made That a Law?

Every country has its fair share of weird laws. The longer their history, the stranger these laws seems to become. Most of them have something interesting to say about the culture and population, but some make you wonder. I often wonder which genius was first to do something that made the government go, "Well, what they did is *technically* not illegal, so, now we have make it an official crime." These are only a handful of the odd laws out there.

☞ In Washington, DC, you can still be prosecuted for being a common scold—a law dating back to the 1800s. A common scold is described in English law as: "a troublesome and angry woman who, by her brawling and wrangling among her neighbors, doth break the public peace, and beget, cherish and increase public discord." In other words? A nasty woman. If you want to know how they were punished, read on.

☞ The next time you are in Zion, Illinois, make sure you don't offer your cigar to any animals who want a puff. It's illegal. A pull of your pipe or cigarette is, however, above board.

☞ It is illegal to cause a nuclear eruption in England. Similarly in China, it is illegal for individuals to store more than a thousand kilograms of explosives in their homes. Who tried that?

☞ It is illegal for frogs to croak after eleven at night in Tennessee. A croaking curfew!

☞ Royals get first pick: in England, it is law that "all beached whales and sturgeons [a type of fish, now protected] must be first offered to the reigning monarch." This law was implemented in 1322.

☞ Swallow it! In Goodyear, Arizona it is "unlawful for any person to spit upon any of the public sidewalks or crosswalks in the city or upon any public path…"

☞ A UK law in the 1872 Licensing Act, states that it is "illegal to be drunk in the pub." You figure that one out!

☞ In Destin, Florida, it is illegal to sell ice cream at a cemetery. Oh, and to drive on the graves. No grave joy riding, you hear?

☞ It is an offense in England and Wales to be drunk while tending a herd of cattle. I can see the slogan now… "Don't drink and herd." For that matter, it is also illegal to be drunk and in charge of a horse.

☞ This will make you really enjoy your next piece of gum: In Singapore, it is illegal to sell gum. Vendors can face fines up to one hundred thousand dollars, plus imprisonment. It is also illegal to chew it, unless you can prove it is for therapeutic reasons. Emotional Support Gum.

☞ Up until 1976, in the UK, there was a law that was part of the 1831 London Hackney Carriage Act, which required all cars to carry at least one bale of hay. Why, you ask? It was originally written for horse-drawn carriages. Eating hay was your horse's version of getting gas.

☞ According to the UK Metropolitan Streets Act of 1867, it is illegal to drive a cow down a roadway between 10 a.m. and 7 p.m. without the permission of the Commissioner of Police first.

☞ Under an 1839 law, you are forbidden to ding-dong ditch in England. In other words, to "willfully and wantonly disturb any inhabitant by pulling or ringing any doorbell or knocking at any door without lawful excuse."

☞ Speaking of disturbances, it is illegal to interrupt a church service in Mississippi. If you do, you can face a fine up to $500, and six months in jail.

☞ Switzerland really does have its head screwed on straight… In recent legislature regarding animal welfare, it became illegal to have just one pet goldfish in a bowl. You *must* have two or more. Since goldfish are social creatures, it is considered animal cruelty to keep this fish in what is essentially solitary confinement. Other animals are also covered in this law, including guinea pigs and budgerigars. Go Swiss!

Embarrassing Deaths

Hugging at the Moon

The Chinese poet Li Po was known to love the drink as much as he loved the written word. One beautiful night in CE 762, he took a ride down the Yangtze River. He was slightly smashed when he saw the dazzling reflection of the moon on the water's surface. He decided to embrace the reflection, falling into the water and drowning.

It might be a *little* embarrassing, but I think this is one of the best ways to go. So poetic. Death by moon hug. It's especially haunting when you read one of his most famous poems, "Drinking Alone." Here is a clip:

> I take my wine jug out among the flowers
>
> to drink alone, without friends.
>
> I raise my cup to entice the moon.
>
> That, and my shadow, makes us three.
>
> But the moon doesn't drink,
>
> and my shadow silently follows.
>
> I will travel with moon and shadow,
>
> happy to the end of spring.
>
> When I sing, the moon dances.
>
> When I dance, my shadow dances, too.
>
> We share life's joys when sober.
>
> Drunk, each goes a separate way.
>
> Constant friends, although we wander,
>
> we'll meet again in the Milky Way.

All Wound Up and Nowhere to Go

Any *Mousehunt* fans out there will find this story especially interesting. Paul Thomas was a forty-seven-year-old man from Connecticut, and the co-owner of a company called George Thomas & Sons Textile. One afternoon in August 1987, while he was operating a pin-wheel dresser machine (which winds woolen yarn from a large spool onto a smaller one) he accidentally fell in.

Before anyone even noticed what had happened, Paul had become wrapped in hundreds of yards of yarn. *Hundreds of yards of yarn.* When tallied, the poor man suffocated to death under eight hundred yards of string. He was pronounced dead at the scene.

If there is anything to be said—besides how awkward and horrible a death that must have been—it's that that was one hell of a machine. It was so lighting fast that witnesses couldn't even see Paul underneath the layers and layers of string.

If you haven't seen the movie *Mousehunt*, go watch it. No one dies by getting wrapped up in a ball of string, but you'll understand why I recommend it once you've seen it. I can't speak for him, but I think Paul would really connect to this line from the movie.

"You used to love string..."

—Lars Smuntz, *Mousehunt*

Lend a Hand, Lose a Head

The Siamese princess, Sunandha Kumariratana, was King Rama V's favorite wife. In Siam, noble men kept many wives and concubines, and her husband was reported to have a whopping eighty-two children. Among the eighty-two, Sunandha had just given birth to a daughter, and had another on the way. Which is why her tragic end is especially distressing and dunderheaded.

In May 1880, Sunandha took her two-year-old daughter and her royal entourage on a trip to one of their mansions, the "Summer Palace," in Bang Pa-In. In order to reach the Summer Palace, they had to cross Chao Phraya River, Siam's biggest. Being royals, Sunandha and her daughter were towed in a separate boat all by themselves.

As they crossed, their boat was swept up in a strong current, and the royal barge tipped over, dumping the princess and her daughter into the churning waters. They cried for help—but her guards and servants watched on, and did nothing, as they slowly drowned. Why didn't they land them a hand? You see, in Siam, it was forbidden to touch a royal, upon pain of death. It was an ancient law, but strictly enforced. So they simply watched on.

The death of his favorite wife, young daughter, and their unborn child was quite hard on poor King Rama, and he imprisoned the guard who failed to give the order to save them. Her funeral procession was one of the most expensive in that country's history, and, as a tribute, he had a statue created of her. He placed it in the gardens at the Summer Palace that poor Princess Sunandha never quite reached, and you can still see it there today.

WHERE IS SIAM?

Before its government transitioned to a constitutional monarchy in 1932, Siam was the name of what we call Thailand today. The name was changed back and forth a few more times, but it became *official* official in 1949. The change was due to political upheaval, and the desire of the country's People's Party to bring Siam into the modern world (i.e. western world). They changed their flag, national anthem, and even their dress. The name Siam comes from the Sanskrit word *śyāma*, meaning dark or brown, meant to represent the skin tone of the people. The name Thailand comes from a Sanskrit word *thai*, meaning "free," but which is also an ethnic group in the country. Thus, it is named *both* the land of the free and the land of Thai people. Two birds with one stone!

Problems with Execution

There's nothing simple about death, but most endings are usually pretty straightforward. The same goes with executions. Public executions were plain and simple, usually. A person came to die, and the executioner did the job. Body: disposed of. Crowd: entertained and/or chastened from the lesson learned. But, as we will see here, sometimes, it wasn't so simple!

She Did It Her Way

Hannah Dagoe was described as a "strong, lusty" Irish woman. The strong part might have been attributed to her physique, but I'd say she had quite a strong character, and would leave a lasting impression on anyone.

In 1763, she was condemned for theft (she literally jacked the entire contents of an old lady's apartment who had befriended her). Once imprisoned, she became "the terror of her fellow-prisoners" and even "stabbed one of the men who had given evidence against her." The guy lived, in case you were wondering.

On the way to her execution, Hannah "showed little concern at her miserable state, and paid no attention to the exhortations of the Romish priest who attended her." As soon as her cart pulled up to the gallows, she managed to quickly unbind her hands, and threw herself at the unprepared executioner in a wild sucker punch—delivering "a blow so violent that she nearly felled him."

Hannah beating down the poor hangman.

She started shouting at him, *daring* him to hang her. Then, to revenge herself upon him, she started ripping off her clothes, and threw the shreds into the crowd. (This wasn't for striptease purposes, but because it was an executioner's right to claim the clothes of his victims as payment—she wasn't going to let him have *nun.*)

After quite the kerfuffle, he finally managed to get the rope around her neck. As soon as he did this, she pulled out a handkerchief, wrapped it around her head, and, in her half-naked state, "threw herself out of the cart, before the signal was given, with such violence that she broke her [own] neck and died instantly." She lived just as she died: her way.

Pole on the Block

Margaret Pole was the daughter of a Duke of England, his brothers were two Plantagenet kings. She was no doubt descended from a long and noble line—but life wasn't destined to be all gowns, gossip, and gout for poor Margaret. When the War of Roses erupted, and power changed hands from her family to the Tudors, the rest of her bloodline was hunted down, just in case they ever dared to reinstate themselves as rulers. As a woman, Margaret was spared, but life was by no means easy for her. The *end* of her life, even less so.

She was constantly suspected of treason, and in 1539, Henry VIII made her conviction final. She was, at the ripe old age of sixty-five, practically a centenarian in those times. Who even has the energy for treason at that age? I'm feeling lazy just thinking about it. Seems like too much work.

Margaret was held in the infamous Tower of London for two and a half long years…just awaiting death. When her execution finally came, it thankfully, was a "private" one, though with numerous witnesses. And it turned out one of the most horrific and *poorly executed* executions in history.

The axe man, it soon became apparent, was completely inexperienced. It might have even been his first execution. He missed with the first swing, gashing her shoulder. He then missed several more times. It took eleven swings to finish the job. He was described as a "blundering youth," who "hacked her head and shoulders to pieces." A cruel, bloody end for Margaret Pole.

All for nothing really. She maintained her innocence until the end. In 1886, she became a Catholic martyr. On the wall of her cell, a poem is carved that is believed to be by her hand:

> For traitors on the block should die;
> I am no traitor, no, not I!
> My faithfulness stands fast and so,
> towards the block I shall not go!
> Nor make one step, as you shall see;
> Christ in Thy Mercy, save Thou me!

I Get Chopped, You Get Chopped

There were certain steps to ensure a swift guillotine execution that any professional executioner would know. Once the victim's head was on the block, their neck would be placed in an iron brace, and the executioner's assistant would pull on their hair to hold the head in place, ready for the blade's fall. But, Monsieur Lacoste, a Frenchman, soon to become the guillotine's next client, was as bald as an egg. So, there was nothing the assistant could do, except hold onto something else. He grasped Lacoste's very small ears.

Just as the blade descended, Lacoste managed to break free of the assistant's hold on his ears, and sank his teeth into the assistant's hand. But that wasn't enough to avoid the guillotine—poor Lacoste's head was chopped. But, after the initial rush of blood flow slowed, the poor executioner's assistant looked down into the basket to see his own severed thumb, stuck between the still-grimacing teeth of M. Lacoste.

We Believed That?

SUPERSTITIONS

*"There is nothing either good or bad,
but thinking makes it so."*

—Shakespeare, *Hamlet*, Act II Scene II

Superstitious Minds

There is physically not enough paper in the world to contain all the superstitions our human race has thought up through the centuries. Probably not even in this past century. And, even if I did try to note them all down, there would be so many different variations—most conflicting and from vague sources—that you would quickly throw this book across the room. You see, folklore varies by culture, century, and even by area. A certain belief in one region will have a completely different twist in another, as you'll soon discover. You simply can't pin them all down. I won't try!

The mysterious and fascinating superstitions here have one main criteria: that they are not commonly known. Now, don't get me wrong, at some point *everyone* hears a whisper of a certain superstition, shrugs their shoulders, and continues living their life. But most don't investigate further, only nerds like me. So, even if you are vaguely aware of a superstition explored in this chapter—maybe, possibly, definitely, certainly, hopefully, you'll learn something new about it. At worst, you'll fill your brain with some cool new information. At best, you'll become extremely superstitious, jumpy, and never go about life the same way again.

Shoeperstition

To the average person, shoes serve a simple purpose: to be worn on feet as protection against the modern elements that litter the floor of our world (chewing gum, dirt, broken glass, Legos, and other things we prefer not to think about). There's nothing mystical about shoes. Nothing to suggest an omen. Nothing going on here. Except…there *is*. And has been for years.

According to centuries of lore, shoes have had a special, er, foothold, in society and culture. The most popular superstition relating to shoes is that they are instruments of *luck*. Particularly, throwing them at people as they leave in order to bring them good fortune. Now, before you throw your shoe at your friend when they leave your house…

The geographical origin of this superstition is not completely clear, though there are roots in Scotland, the Isle of Man, various regions of Scandinavia, and other parts of Europe. The histories are chock-full of stories and literature about this belief. Here are a few examples— note that these are all from the UK, though there are many more from other areas as well.

The famed British poet, Alfred Tennyson, writes in his collection, *English Idyls and Other Poems*:

> For this thou shalt from all things seek,
>
> Marrow of mirth and laughter,
>
> And wheresoe'er thou move, good luck,
>
> Shall throw her old shoe after.

Comedic poet, actor, and playwright Ben Johnson wrote, simply:

> Hurl after me a shoe,
>
> I'll be merry whatever I'll do.

Also, the English writer, John Heywood, best known for his poems and proverbs, wrote in his "Luck Song and Dance of the Olde Shooe":

> And home again hitherward quick as a bee,
>
> Now for good luck, cast an old shoe at me.

In all these examples, throwing a shoe bestows good luck upon the assaulted. But, there are other sources where throwing shoes at newlywed couples, specifically, was a common practice.

In English writer William Hone's *The Table-Book* (1827), a correspondent named Morley from Leeds wrote about this custom happening in Yorkshire, which he did not recall having seen before, nor know the origins of.

"It is called 'trashing,'" he writes, "which signifies pelting people with old shoes on their return from church on the wedding-day." He also notes it was usually practiced among the "lower orders" with turf-sod (grass and soil) or mud being substituted if shoes were in short supply—and generally thrown in a lighthearted, joking way. Morley then continues by delving into the word itself. Why was it called "trashing"? According to his musings:

> "Although it is true that an old shoe is to this day called 'a trash,' yet it did not, certainly, give the name to the nuisance. To 'trash' originally signified, to clog, incumber, or impede the progress of anyone. [...] But why old shoes in particular were selected as the missiles most proper for impending the progress of new married persons, it is now perhaps impossible to discover."

Why indeed, if his thinking is correct, would well-wishers want to impede a new couples' progress? We may never know the exact origins. It is important to note, though, that this ritual was not always limited to just weddings. The same custom was applied to someone going on a long journey, or a ship leaving port, in order to give them luck, and a safe return.

Punch cartoon, 1854, depicting Queen Victoria "Throwing the Old Shoe" after her soldiers as they departed for the Crimean War.

There may be another explanation concerning marriage, however. This ritual could be descended from an ancient rite dealing with the transfer of property, since women were regarded as such in many of the countries where this practice is believed to have originated. There is even a biblical reference to the practice in the Old Testament, in Ruth 4: 7 (NKJV):

> Now this was the custom in former times in Israel concerning redeeming and exchanging, to confirm anything: one man took off his sandal and gave it to the other, and this was a confirmation in Israel.

Expanding on this theory, in Anglo-Saxon marriages, it was common practice was for a bride's father to deliver her shoe to her soon-to-be husband, who would then touch her on the head with it to symbolize his authority over her. Though some accounts state is was less of a "touch" and more of a blow to the head. (Cringe.)

A professor of folklore at the University of Hertfordshire in England, Dr. Ceri Houlbrook, was shopping for wedding season when she noticed a packet of shoe-shaped confetti in the aisle. The confetti sparked her interest, and led her on a search for its potential basis in folklore. What she discovered were its ties to luck, authority, but also, its connection to magic. Possessing someone's shoe was believed to give you great power over them. "In 1644," Houlbrook writes, "there was a Scottish witchcraft trial in which the purported sorcerer Patrick Malcolm was accused of trying to acquire a woman's left shoe in order to control her and force her to follow him." There is no doubt, the shoe contains heavy symbolism. Luckily, nowadays, people simply tie shoes to the back of the "Just Married" car.

While we're still on the topic of throwing stuff, there's one other thing thrown at weddings, but it's much less brutal, and more well-known: rice. Many are familiar with this grain being tossed at newlyweds as they depart for their honeymoon. It is likely meant to symbolize prosperity, since it has the feeling of rain, which is always seen as celebratory, and a sign of fertility. But, what is thrown differs in other cultures. Ancient Romans once tossed wheat, later, this became rice; Italian weddings sometimes end with candy or sweet nuts being thrown, and in Morocco, raisins. Of all the theories, this "prosperity" factor is most likely what that ties the shoe-throwing ritual together.

Omens of the Future

Many once believed that mistakenly putting your left shoe on your right foot was an omen of bad luck coming your way. Some still do! Also, according to the 1846 book, *Current Superstitions*, the *order* in which you put your shoes on matters too:

To clothe the left foot before the right foot is a sign of misfortune.

The state of your shoe could even predict your future. Shoes are very personal items, taking on the essence of the wearer through time. So, old shoes would contain your essence even more, and thus were more likely to show you your future. Here is an ancient rhyme about this superstition:

> Wear out the toe, live to see woe
>
> Wear out the side, live to be a bride
>
> Wear out the ball, live to see all
>
> Wear out the heel, you'll save a good deal!

There are many variations on this verse, of course, changing by area, and even year to year. For example, a variation of the second line, "Wear out the side, you'll be a rich bride."

Just one more thing about shoes and weddings that sort of fits nicely (if that's the right word) into this doom and gloom section.

When a couple are married and are driving off, if old shoes are thrown after them for good luck, and one of the shoes lodges on the coach or carriage, it is a sign that one of the party will die before the year is out. (Waltham, Massachusetts)

Idioms or Shoe-dioms

The Shoe Is on the Other Foot

I'm sure you've heard the idiom "the shoe (or boot) is on the other foot." There's also the "wrong" foot. This is usually said when situations have been reversed or circumstances have changed. The phrase stems from the 1800s, but still has life in modern times—I even heard it while travelling recently in South Carolina. Winston Churchill also used this phrase in his 1908 book, *My African Journey*,

which chronicles his eye-opening tour of East Africa: "Here…
the boot is on the other leg, and Civilization is ashamed of her
arrangements in the presence of a savage." This region of Africa was
just beginning to show the encroaching influence of the West, and
the "normal" cultural influences he was used to were starting to look
completely foreign, and even invasive, to his eyes. This demonstrates
the jarring feeling that comes with a reversal of fortune or perspective.

Me Meté la Pata

In many Hispanic cultures, frequently heard in my hometown,
Miami, another common saying is "*me meté la pata*" or "*me dí la pata.*"
This roughly translates to "I put my foot in it" which means—for
lack of a better expression—I messed up—in a pretty embarrassing
way. You might use this if you spoiled a surprise party or, if you live
in Miami, at every awkward moment (i.e. every five minutes). Of
course, this idiom isn't necessarily related to "shoes," but is worth
mentioning, because…well…I guess I don't have a valid reason.
Maybe I shouldn't have mentioned it. Oops. ¡Me meté la pata!

Goody, Goody

I think we've all called someone (or been called) a goody two shoes
at one point in our lives, even if we've only said it secretly in our
minds. But, if you live under a rock, or you're an alien visiting Earth
for the first time, and have never heard this expression—first of all,
welcome—and second, this means an excessively virtuous person.
Someone who seems so good that they're almost *too* good. Or, as my
little brother says, "trying too hard." Tracing its origin is simple. In
1765, John Newberry published a children's book called *Goody Two-
Shoes*, which popularized this phrase. The story has similarities to that
of Cinderella. It follows an orphan girl, who goes through life with
only one shoe, and, despite her troubles, shows heart and is virtuous.

Then, one day, a rich gentleman gives her a brand-new pair of shoes all for her own, bringing her complete joy. Later in life, she achieves some wealth of her own, proving that being "good" will always be rewarded.

Put Yourself in My Shoes

There are always variations of idioms, this one being no exception. "Put yourself in my/her/his shoes" is also "walk a day in my shoes" or "walk a mile in my shoes" and other variations, depending on the situation. It can be easily explained as seeing a situation or even life itself from the perspective of another. Shoes have long been considered to contain the essence of the wearer. They are shaped by our experiences, travels, body, and the ground we trod upon. In this way, the meaning of this idiom is perfect.

Waiting for the Other Shoe to Drop

This idiom means that a situation is going better than expected, but there is still an expectation that the good won't last, and fate will change for the worse on a dime. In other words—feeling something is too good to be true.

You Have Big Shoes to Fill

In one of my favorite movies, *The Devil Wears Prada*, this phrase is spoken by the character Emily (played by Emily Blunt) to an intimidated, newbie secretary named Andrea (played by Anne Hathaway). I considered explaining all the details of why Emily said this to the new girl, but instead, will simply encourage you to watch this movie if you haven't! This idiom means the person has to make a great deal of effort to measure up to their predecessor.

If the Shoe Fits, Wear It

This idiom's meaning has morphed, as every language and dialect tends to do. Originally, it was intended to help someone accept criticism. For example, if my friend tells me I'm one of those people who is bad at answering their phone, my mom my tell me, "If the shoe fits, wear it." But, it can also refer to a situation, truth, or likeness. If you hate doing math, but are a math genius, someone might say this phrase to you. If you are of the same ilk, or if something is meant to be. This phrase has likely originated from—you guessed it—Cinderella! She gains everything once the famous glass shoe is found to fit only her.

Charms

The number of charms surrounding shoes are impossible to round up completely, so I've only featured a few true gems here. They range from simply placing your shoes a certain way, to incantations and rituals that resemble those of Wicca.

A Toss of Fate

You don't just throw salt over your shoulder, but shoes and horseshoes too! And, in the historical records pertaining to this, it was all in how the shoe landed. If you threw a horseshoe over your shoulder, and it landed a certain way (facing you in the shape of a U), it was your lucky day. Having the "horn" parts of a horseshoe face you (like a lowercase n) was thought to bring terrible fortune. In the Scottish Highlands, an annual custom involving shoes was thought to be prophetic. On Halloween, it was customary for people to throw a shoe over their house. The direction it pointed when it landed was the path that should be traveled next. But if it landed with the sole facing upward—bad luck, lass.

Warding Off Evil

Shoes were believed to provide protection—not just from the dirty ground, but from evil. To avoid evil spirits, Reginald Scot advised a charm in his 1584 work, *Discovery of Witchcraft*: "spit in the shoe of your right foot when putting it on; and that Vairus saith is good and wholesome to do before you go into a dangerous place." His book was intended as an exposé of witchcraft, and is chock full of the most fascinating (to modern eyes) charms and spells—if you ever get the chance, it's free online, so look it up!

Nighttime Charms

In England, placing your shoes in the shape of a T under your bed before going to sleep was a charm used to predict a girl's future husband. Hopefully, they would dream of their man's face that night.

Once the shoes were in place, and before lying in bed, the girls were instructed to say:

> I place my shoes in the form of a T,
>
> Trusting my true love this night to see,
>
> And learn what like my spouse will be.
>
> This is another interesting variation on the above. I would really love to see someone sleeping with a stocking on their head.
>
> Point your shoes towards the street,
>
> Leave your garters on your feet,
>
> Put your stockings on your head,
>
> You'll dream of the man you are going to wed.

Another similar nighttime charm: elderly individuals would place their shoes in the shape of a cross, V, or T under the bed in order to heal rheumatism.

Love Charms

These charms come from the lovely book, *Current Superstitions*, by Fanny Bergen. It is bursting with charms, superstitions, and ancient rituals for the passionate, nerdy scholar (not me, I swear). It is in the public domain, so, available at no charge, and I highly encourage further reading if this subject interests you. As you can see, many charms have small variations:

> When the call of the first turtle-dove is heard, sit down and remove the shoe and stocking from the left foot, turn the stocking inside out, in the heel of which if a hair is found, it

will be of the color of the hair of the future husband or wife.
(Tennessee)

If the finder of a four-leaved clover put it in her own shoe, she
will marry the first person with whom she crosses a bridge.
(Michigan)

Wear a piece of fern in the toe of your shoe, and the first
person you meet, you will marry. (New Hampshire; a
variation on the above)

If you walk with a gentleman (for the first time), and have
on new shoes, and go over a bridge, you will marry him.
(Eastern Massachusetts)

THE STORIES AND LEGENDS ABOUT SHOES

Cinderella

During the Middle Ages, the beloved story of Cinderella and her
shoe was born. Many of the superstitions about shoes also began
during this era. We all know the story—a magical evening where
one mysterious belle loses her shoe, and is searched for high and
low, finally being discovered by, and reunited with her true love.

The Wizard of Oz

Her name is synonymous with those dazzling, sparkling red shoes:
Dorothy. When she clicked her heels together three times, she
returned home. Now, whenever someone wears red shoes or sparkly
shoes, one can't help but think of her.

The Three Kings

Most Christians, Roman Catholics, and Latin Americans know of
this ritual, though other cultures and faiths might be familiar with it
as well. On Three Kings Day, also called the Feast of the Epiphany,
children leave their shoes outside by the front door in hopes that
the Three Kings will leave gifts in their shoes. The actual day this
happens is on the twelfth day of Christmas.

There Was an Old Woman Who Lived in a Shoe

We can say this classic nursery rhyme is simply about an old woman (who lived in a shoe) with too many children. But since we're talkin' folklore, some believe her story symbolizes fruitfulness, because of the ancient connection between fertility and shoes.

Other Shoes Uses—Heads Up!

Like many superstitions, crumbs have floated down over the centuries to show themselves in various cultures and in different ways. Usually, there is a way to trace an origin, as we've discussed. Though, sometimes, shoes have shown up in society for reasons unrelated to those we've talked about.

If you do a search, you'll see that shoe-throwing has also been practiced simply to deliver a message—to make your feelings about someone clear. But this isn't so much about superstition as it is likely that shoes are heavy and chunky and beg to be thrown in the heat of anger. In the year 359, the Roman Emperor Contantius II was giving a speech to a group of Limigantes, trying to gain their loyalty, when someone in the crowd threw a shoe at him, shouting "*marha, marha.*" One rough translation likens this to "blockhead" (i.e. stupid person).

In modern times, shoe-throwing has been used for this type of protestation too. There have been numerous incidents over the years, and in countries all over the world, such as Australia, India, Taiwan, the US, UK, Hong Kong, Pakistan, and more, where shoe-throwing incidents have been recorded. They've been thrown at criminals, public officials, and *especially* politicians. Depending on where you live, this might be the only shoe-throwing you'll see in modern day.

The Shoe's Journey

To recap, shoes have a unique and varied history. They have been linked to luck, fertility and prosperity, and have become symbolic as an extension of ourselves. The folklore, mysticism, and ritual surrounding shoes is rich. They were used at weddings, to pelt the bride and groom for good luck and fertility; also, in modernity, they are tied to the backs of honeymoon cars. They were used for charms and for fortune-telling. And nowadays, are thrown at people in protest or in anger. There are tons of stories, nursery rhymes, idioms, and folklore surrounding shoes—and, now that your brain is full of this information, you'll start to notice it a lot more!

To make another bad, nonsensical dad joke—we have now walked a mile in the superstitious history of shoes. I hope you enjoyed the journey! I'll stop now.

WHAT DO YOU KNOW ABOUT SUPERSTITIONS?

- ☞ It's bad luck to cut your nails on a Friday. (Pigeon Cove, Massachusetts)

- ☞ If you cut your nails on a Sunday, you'll do something shameful before the week is out. (Maine)

- ☞ To look over another person's shoulder in the looking glass means disappointment. (Deer Isle, Maine)

- ☞ If you dry the extreme tip of a calf's tongue, and carry it in your pocket, you will always have some money in your purse.

- ☞ Entering a house with your left foot first will bring bad luck to those who live there.

Burn, Baby, Burn

Some superstitions are so deeply ingrained in our lives that we don't even give them a second thought, let alone consider them "superstitions." They just *are*. This is the case with superstitions about our baby teeth.

When a baby tooth falls out, in Western cultures, it's considered an exciting occasion—your child is growing—and the child is told to put their tooth under their pillow, or on their nightstand. Then, when they are asleep, the "tooth fairy" will come, and take it away. Sometimes, the tooth fairy even leaves a gift in return! This is usually money, candy, or some small token. If we're being honest…I'll admit that, sometimes, I pulled a loose tooth out before it was ready, just for the money. Don't judge.

If this tooth fairy practice is familiar to you, you've probably taken it for granted your whole life. I don't blame you—so have I!

A probable origin that explains this practice is that it was meant to *appease* the fairy realm. Folklore is full of stories of parents fearing that their children would be stolen by trolls or fairies. And, in order to appease them, and protect their children, parents would leave a tooth out as an offering while they slept.

This custom is traced back to the thirteenth century, and is written about in two Medieval Icelandic literary works known collectively as *Edda*. These works probably originated even earlier during the Viking age. *Edda* were the first written records of Norse and Northern European traditions. This custom is called *tand-fé* or tooth fee. It stated that a child is paid when they lose their first tooth. Funnily enough, Norse warriors would also pay children for their teeth when going into battle, since baby teeth were considered lucky.

THE TOOTH FAIRY AROUND THE WORLD

In modern Spanish and Hispanic cultures, the tooth fairy is a called a small rat or mouse (because they are usually unseen and blamed for disappearing things such as cheese). The common name for them is "*Ratoncito Pérez*" (translated to "little Pérez mouse") or even "*el Ratón de los Dientes*" (meaning "the tooth mouse"). This little guy even has his very own museum in Madrid.

France also has a little mouse instead of a proper tooth fairy. In this lovely country it is called: "*La Bonne Petite Souris*," translating to "the good little mouse." There is a short fairytale, written by Madame d'Aulnoy, by the same name if you're looking for something to read your children. There is also a three-part children's play, simply titled, *The Tooth Fairy*, by Esther Watkins Arnold.

Also, I would be foolish if I didn't mention the comedy movies *The Tooth Fairy*, and *The Tooth Fairy 2*, starring Dwayne "the Rock" Johnson, and Larry the Cable Guy, respectively. Definitely not for research purpose, but for giggle purposes.

The tooth fairy doesn't really visit South Africa (plane fare, ugh), but children put their shoes inside of their slippers in this part of the world.

Oh, and let's not forget—August 22 is National Tooth Fairy Day in America! What is my recommended celebration tactic? Go to the dentist.

Salty Tooth

During the Middle Ages, new superstitions began to emerge about baby teeth. In the north of Britain, it was customary to burn them, after sprinkling them with salt. The reason for this was to protect them for the child in the afterlife. People thought that if their teeth were not destroyed on earth, they would spend an eternity in the hereafter looking for their owner. One man from Lancashire remembers being told as a boy that the consequence for not burning a fallen tooth was: "to search for it in a pail of blood, in hell, after death." Pretty rough, eh?

One girl from Tunstall, Staffordshire, in England wrote: "I tell everyone that I am not superstitions, and I tell myself that I am not, but sometimes, I wonder, because if one of my teeth came out, I would not think of burning it without smothering it in salt first." It's interesting to note that she only considered the salt part superstitious! Not burning her teeth.

But why salt? Well, it was widely used as a preservative for food, and was considered a powerful, protective element. It's fair to assume the salt preserved the tooth until the person died, and provided better protection than the tooth had by itself.

If you didn't burn your teeth, though, another option was to keep them safe in a jar. People believed that once you reached heaven, you had to account for all your missing teeth, and (if applicable) any amputated limbs. That is why many have been buried with their jar of teeth. In Derbyshire, one woman named Abby remembered her grandmother calling out at funerals saying, "Have you got his teeth in the coffin?" or "Don't bury him without his teeth." If you had an amputated limb, though—there was no need to keep it creepily stored away somewhere—it was simply buried.

Another reason for this custom is because it protected you from witchcraft. It's a common belief that if someone possesses some part of you—a tooth, fingernail, hair, *shoe*, etc.—they had power over you. This belief is not as far-fetched as it may seem—many Wiccan spells and rituals list these materials in the ingredients.

One more yummy method to get rid of your teeth was to feed them to animals or rodents. It was believed the new-grown adult teeth would take the shape of the animal that ate the baby teeth. Why, you ask? The parents hoped that their kids' adult teeth would grow hard and sharp!

Lastly, in Wales and even some Middle Eastern countries, there is a practice of *throwing* your tooth. Some say over your shoulder, others up at the sun, some at the ground, on top of a roof—the list goes on. Again, this begs explanation. Like so many traditions, it's likely rooted in ancient paganism—to give an offering.

◆

Most superstitions come about for mysterious reasons, but I believe a lot are born to simply give us comfort. The unknown is scary. Also… change, misfortune, mystery—these make us edgy. It's just easier to have some action to protect us or something to blame for misfortunes.

In fact, this reason might explain this entire book. Dare I say, human nature itself. Inventions, medical cures, superstitions, etc.—they all have a purpose in appeasing our needs. A promise everything will be all right.

Losing your teeth is painful and confusing if you're a child. It certainly was for me. Adults giving kids something magical and exciting to look forward to…well, who can blame us?

You *Can* Touch This

Gone are the days when monarchs were thought of as near gods, but history does chronicle these lovely ages in detail for us to smile back upon. A common healing superstition that existed in the time when rulers were thought of as divine was called the "royal touch," or "king's touch."

In this ritual, mainly performed by the French and English, the monarchs would "touch their subjects, regardless of social classes,

with the intent to cure them of various diseases and conditions."
Perhaps we can imagine a Disney World-esque line of suffering
subjects stretching around the castle with groans, coughing, and
general pain—all waiting for the touch of a king or queen (just not the
animated kind in a body suit).

A common part of this practice was the gifting of a gold medal
with a religious engraving on it. The monarch would put it around
the subject's neck, and tell them to wear it constantly, so that the
healing treatment worked properly. But, as you might expect, many
people seeking the royal touch didn't necessarily believe in it, but
wanted the gold in order to pawn it. Perhaps this was the reason for
its long-standing popularity? My guess is the sick person traded it
to purchase actual medicine (though hopefully not the kind in the
medical attention chapter of this book!). Who do you think is more
scoundrel-y? The monarch for their airs, or the cunning subject?

King Henri II of France, who many
remember as an ambitious monarchist,
is pictured "healing" a young man here.

Rulers from "bloody" Mary I of England to Charles II of France were all known to have performed this "laying on of hands" ritual. Often, it was used as a tool to establish a ruler's legitimacy if their throne wasn't completely secure.

If you are a literature lover like me, you'll be tickled to see that Shakespeare described this same tradition in Act IV of *Macbeth*:

> A most miraculous work in this good king;
> Which often, since my here-remain in England,
> I have seen him do. How he solicits heaven,
> Himself best knows: but strangely-visited people,
> All swoln and ulcerous, pitiful to the eye
> The mere despair of surgery, he cures,
> Hanging a golden stamp about their necks,
> Put on with holy prayers: and 'tis spoken
> To the succeeding royalty he leaves
> The healing benediction

Finally (*cough*, I mean eventually), this practice began dying out in the early 1700s, becoming essentially nonexistent by the end of the century. The popular poet and physician Sir Richard Blackmore even praised King's William III and George I for abandoning such as "superstitious and insignificant ceremony," which he firmly believed was a "Papish" plot.

While we're still on the subject, yes, this is indeed still a common practice in the spiritual and religious world. The "laying on of hands" is performed all over the world by spiritual leaders. Though, I haven't heard anything yet about gold coins coming with the deal.

King Charles I of England giving the king's touch to a young subject
with scrofulous (i.e. tuberculosis).

Fast Facts

☞ Saint Edward the Confessor (1042–1066), one of the last
Anglo-Saxon kings in England, was said to be the first monarch
who possessed the healing power of the royal touch.

☞ The royal touch was usually performed on holy days for a
greater chance of success.

☞ Charles II of England has the highest touch record with over
9,200 people (does Guinness know?).

☞ The ruler's hands were usually anointed with blessed oil,
believed to give them the power.

☞ The ceremony was officially removed from the Book of
Common Prayer in 1732.

The Banana Curse

While we are still talking about contagious superstitions, this seems like a good time to address one that is widely shared among sailors, captains, fishermen, and other sea-bound individuals: the banana curse. As much as this sounds like the name of an episode on the kids show *Dora the Explorer*, the fear surrounding this superstition began long ago, and still exists today.

The gist of it: having bananas on board your ship is bad luck. Fatal luck, even. Whether a large cargo ship, dinghy, or fishing boat—no seafaring vessel is immune—this tropical fruit is a no-no and can easily get you thrown off board if you're caught with one.

The origin of this superstition begins in the early 1700s, at the peak of trade between the Spanish empire and the Caribbean. And, if you have been near a dock or fishing boat yourself lately, you'll know this superstition hasn't died out in the least. There are many possible causes behind this that ultimately cemented it in seafaring minds, despite the passing of centuries. Let's peel back the layers one at a time.

The Case for Vanishing Ships

At the height of the trading boom, many ships went missing. Understandable. With so many safety hazards to account for at sea—bad weather, piracy, running aground, floating adrift—it wasn't uncommon that some ships were never seen again after leaving the harbor.

As luck (or lack thereof) would have it, many of the ships that disappeared during this time were carrying a load of cargo that happened to include...*bananas*. Thus two and two were put together, linking this tropical fruit to misfortune. Though it's interesting to note, sources don't specifically name any of the lost ships responsible for this belief, leading us to conclude this "disappearing ship" factor is more rumor than a reason.

THE SHIP-SINKING BANDIT

Just for fun, let's explore some of the most well-known ship disappearances and sinkings over the ages. The list is long, so these are only a few. Again, though history doesn't specifically state that every one of these was carrying the forbidden yellow fruit on board, I think all signs most definitely point to banana. Obviously.

☞ One disappearance which was deemed "the greatest maritime mystery of all time" surrounds the English ship, *Mary Celeste*. But this "disappearance" in 1872 is unique among its kind because the ship itself didn't disappear—just the people on board. The *Mary Celeste* was discovered as a ghost ship off the coast of the Azores, an autonomous region of Portugal, with over six months' worth of food and cargo virtually untouched. Further, there were no signs of it having been attacked or of foul play—all valuables and personal possessions were in the same places their owners had left them. It was almost as if their bodies were spirited away. The only thing remotely out of place was that the ship's lifeboat was missing. This left us with the only reasonable conclusion for the disappearance, that, for some unforeseen reason, the crew and passengers abandoned ship. A perfectly good, all-in-order ship. Maybe they simply went...bananas. (Sorry I had to just once!)

☞ The *USS Wasp* was a 117-foot-long privateering ship whose main mission was to sink British vessels during the War of 1812. With only a year left in the war, in 1814, a Swedish vessel made contact with the ship as it was sailing toward the Caribbean. Little did they know, their eyes would be the last to ever see the *USS Wasp*. Neither the ship, nor the crew of 173 were ever seen again. Bananas being a tropical fruit (and the Caribbean a tropical locale) well, unless the Bermuda Triangle was to blame for the disappearance, it's not such a big leap for already-superstitious sailors to attribute its demise to bananas, right?

The *USS Wasp* doing what it did best.

☞ It's been over two hundred years, but the schooner *Patriot* still generates interest and debate today. In 1812, the northbound ship had just completed a privateering voyage in the tropics, and was rumored to have bounty aboard. In pirate speak: lots of booty in the hold! Might they have also been carrying a particular smile-shaped fruit native to the tropics? Well, on their way north, off the coast of North Carolina, the ship and crew vanished without a trace. Years of debate and speculation over the cause has not led us closer to a definite answer. Some say it fell victim to the pirate Dominique You (a.k.a. "The Bloody Babe"), or that it was attacked by raiders called the Carolina "bankers." Rather bad luck in any case. Could it possibly have been caused by the banana curse, if they indeed had them on board? As the wisdom of Tootsie Pop states: the world may never know.

☞ Last but certainly not least, the sinking of the *Titanic* is another misfortune that can be attributed to the banana. Yes, you read that right. While, of course, there is the small factor of the iceberg to consider, this famous ship *was* carrying a load of at least a thousand bananas on board at the time that it sank. Over a thousand bananas. Reckless, one might say.

TITANIC

Quick Spidery Deaths

Have you ever thrown fruit away—like the skin of an orange, an apple core, or a banana peel—and found your trashcan swarmed by flies? If you live anywhere with a warm climate, you've likely experienced this many times before. Fruit attracts insects, poisonous snakes, vermin, and other critters. That's the simple consequence of being so sweet and delicious.

With this in mind, imagine packing boxes upon boxes of fruit into a crowded space with little ventilation, and being confined with it for days, if not a month or more. The critters that found their way into the fruit would most likely find their way to you, too. Especially spiders.

Yes, the insect most attracted to bananas happens to be spiders, and often, their bites were (and are) lethal. After hitching a ride in the banana holds, they would eventually find their way out into the ship. There isn't much room to roam freely on a ship. Many sailors sharing space with these evil castaways would eventually get bitten by deadly spiders or snakes, and die quick, painful deaths. Of all the possible causes for the root of this superstition, as a registered scaredy cat, I favor this one the most.

Too Much Junk In the Hold

There are four routes we can follow when blaming heavy, overburdened cargo holds as the cause for sinking ships, and for general banana misfortune. First, to increase profit, trading vessels would often get stuffed with as much cargo as they could contain. So, if there were any incidents at sea, a heavy ship would double the odds and speed of sinking, not leaving any time to get help. Then, if another ship came upon the remains…you can imagine the crew's thoughts when all that was left in the wreck's wake was a trail of floating bananas.

Similar to weight of cargo, speed was an issue. In order to get their products to buyers without spoilage, ships had to travel quite fast. Faster than was probably safe, considering how much they loaded on board. Hasty travel may have led to hasty mistakes, damaging the ship. We all know what happened to the *Titanic* when it reached an unsafe speed in order to get to its destination.

Next, if you've ever put a banana in a paper bag to ripen it, well, stuffing them into small wooden spaces does about the same thing. But, what's important to note is that, when bananas decompose, they release methane and other toxins into the air, which can create a contaminated environment if there isn't adequate ventilation, and, in extreme cases, can cause asphyxiation. Bad bananas. *Bad* bananas.

Fourth, and finally, if a ship is traveling fast, it is harder for fishermen to catch many fish, isn't it? And when this happens, whether in the eighteenth century or yesterday, it's always attributed to *bad luck*. Not too hard to make the fruity connection, right?

Hawaiian Mythology

Next, we leave the realm of evidence-based guesswork, and enter another realm entirely. One with less reason and more mysticism. Hawaiian mythology has something to say about bananas. But, there are two different takes on it: one of bad luck, the other simply a reminder.

For the first, as Captain Joe Wenegenofsky writes in his article, "The Forbidden Fruit," the whole of which covers this very subject:

> "According to the ancient islanders, bananas were deemed fruits of the gods and looked at as a delicacy. Therefore, a fisherman attempting to catch fish with bananas in the boat would be considered covetous. Such an act of marked greed would warrant no blessing from the gods and most likely render the fisherman fishless."

However, on the other hand, it's been said that when Hawaiian fishermen would take their boats out for long fishing trips, they would tie bananas to the sides, in order to eat, and sustain themselves for the journey. When the bananas started to over-ripen and grew too brown, this was a reminder that the fishermen had been away from home too long, and should head back. This might be interpreted as ill luck, because it signals the ending of a voyage, but also good luck, because one is returning home.

◆

We've covered the major possible reasons for this undying superstition. (There are many more, I'm sure, each different depending on who you ask.) So, let's look at how it has evolved, and what people have said about it.

As Captain Joe Wenegenofsky states, this curse is "the best known and widely disputed" of all the sea-based superstitions (and that's really saying something, because there are quite a lot!).

It has evolved in our modern era to apply mainly to fishing. If you do a quick search online, you will see dozens, if not hundreds, of people bemoaning their ill luck fishing—before finding someone had ignorantly brought a banana aboard, then, disposing of the fruit (and sometimes the culprit, too), and *then* catching loads of fish. Or, you'll find photos of people with a sense of humor, bringing bunches upon bunches of bananas on board for *good* luck. The superstition is certainly alive in one way or another.

According to what Wenegenofsky's seen in his time as a captain, some believers have gone so far as to prohibit *anything* remotely related to the b-word on their vessels. This includes Banana Boat sunscreen, clothing from Banana Republic, banana-flavored muffins—you name it! Often, he has seen "instances where bananas have been forcibly ripped out of an angler's hand or cooler, and flung overboard."

The *New York Times* quoted another captain, named Rick Etzel of Montauk on this issue, saying "…people take the banana thing very seriously. A few years back, a guy on one of my charters showed up wearing a Banana Republic T-shirt. Another guy in the group went up to him with a knife and slashed the logo."

It's is also common to see anti-banana signs along docks, on T-shirts, and even in contracts for crewmembers, fishermen, captains, etc. Some contracts require employees to affirm they would *never* bring one aboard.

But, if you think farms and fruit companies have heeded this fear and have forgone shipping their bananas, you would be wrong, my friend. But, we should keep in mind the advances in *refrigeration* technology.

This is the origin and evolution of the banana curse. I have just one question for you now. Will you ever look at a banana the same way again?

Flower Power

Flowers are beautiful. They're delicate, exotic, and some would even say, erotic. It's no mystery why they are closely linked to human reproduction. One of the most popular flowers in this superstition is the orchid. Its very name comes from the Greek word for testicles: *orkhis*. This is because of its appearance, although the sexual organs of both genders have been represented symbolically by this flower. (While we're on the subject, many natural objects get their names simply because of their physical similarities, which is why "avocado" is the Aztec word for testicle, too.) I swear, this is the last time I'll write testicle. *Testicle.*

Anyway, ancient Greeks believed that an orchid flower could influence the gender of their unborn children, if one of the expectant parents ate part it. If you are unfamiliar with the plant, some orchids grow tubers at the root. The ancient Greeks believed that if the male partner ate the largest tuber, their child would be male. If the parents wanted a female child, the woman would eat the smallest tuber.

Let's put sexism aside, and take a deeper look at why this superstition existed. For one, the orchid has captivated our imaginations for centuries. It is one of the most popular flowers in the world. Throughout history, it has been used for food, medicine, décor, and as an aphrodisiac.

Even the flower itself has developed strategies to ensure pollination. It has a large and diverse family, with over one hundred thousand hybrids! It's practically a reproduction machine. For this very reason, I would call it the floral mascot for fertility.

The first century CE Greek physician, Dioscorides, theorized in his *Materia Medica* that orchids influenced sexuality. Unsurprisingly, it has been a popular gift for new and expecting couples for generations. But let's get real—if you look around the home of anyone over the age of thirty (single or with a partner), odds are, you'll see an orchid somewhere. Maybe three. Who knows why? The people of ancient

China and Japan believed this flower was the symbol of human beauty and perfection. Confucius compared its perfume to the delights of friendship. Also, for decades, it was a very expensive and sought-after flower, since it only grew in tropical locales.

Perhaps for these reasons it has become a status symbol, almost a talisman for prosperity. In any case, the orchid has a lot going for it. Its symbolism has pervaded cultures around the world, and it still maintains a high status—it *does* look quite elegant, you must admit. If you want to get pulled into a serious black hole, researching superstitions about reproduction and pregnancy will take you there. The beautiful orchid is only one petal among them!

Three's a Curse

Lucky numbers. Which one popped into your head when you read that? Was it five? Twenty-three? Seventeen? Everyone has some association with a lucky number. I'll admit it—mine is fifteen. But what about...*unlucky* numbers? Culture and folklore are overflowing with superstitions about them.

The one I find the most interesting is "the rule of three." For ages, it has been considered terrible luck to have three lit candles on a theater stage or in a dressing room. If there were, whoever was closest to the shortest candle would either be the first to die, or the first to marry (talk about options).

There are a few possible origins for the candle superstition. First, too many lit candles increased the risk of fire and, since most theaters were made of wood, this meant a loss of livelihood for the cast if it burned down. Also, there was an early Christian custom of allowing only clergymen to light three candles. This is tied to the representation of the trinity of Father, Son, and Holy Spirit. An unordained person doing so could be seen as sacrilege. But, with the invention of electricity, candle usage melted away, causing this superstition to flicker and snuff out. (Yes, I challenged myself to see how many puns I could fit into one sentence.)

Just the same, it has also been seen as bad luck to light three cigarettes from one match. This comes from when the British fought in the Boer war. When soldiers in the trenches burned a match long enough to ignite three cigarettes, it could be seen by enemy forces. Whoever was last to light their cigarette, "the third man," would then usually be killed by a sniper. Methinks this particular superstition was born as a cautionary tale.

Despite popular belief, the Swedish match maker, Ivar Kreuger, didn't have anything to do with the origin of this superstition—but he certainly benefited and milked it for all it was worth. Think of it—the more matches you used, the more he would sell! Three cigarettes to one match simply wasn't good for business. Preying on people's superstitious natures is too easy.

I must admit—this superstition "struck me" as completely counterintuitive. Isn't the number three supposed to be *good* luck? It is considered a perfect number. "Three times a charm" and all? There is also three wishes granted, the Holy Trinity, the three jewels of Buddhism, the Triple Goddess, etc. The number three is symbolic throughout many cultures.

There is a common saying connected to this superstition, however: "bad luck comes in threes," "death comes in threes," or "never two without three." It's also connected to the idiom "When it rains, it pours." Countless personal accounts report how one grandparent died, quickly followed by an uncle or cousin, and everyone began eyeing other family members to see who might be next. It's been said by psychologists that our minds are simply obsessed with series, and finding an end to ill fortune.

UNLUCKY NUMBER ROULETTE

☞ It's unlucky to have an odd number of people sitting at a table.

☞ If someone has luck three times in one day, it is considered an auspicious day, and any business venture is sure to be successful.

☞ A Scot won't begin anything on May 3, which is called the "Dismal Day."

☞ Numbers ending in three, nine, twelve, or seven are the most likely to strike luck.

☞ To find nine peas in a pod is good luck.

☞ The American two-dollar bill is considered unlucky, but if one tears a small piece off the corner, its safe. Why? Because a torn corner makes a triangle which has three points—a "lucky" number. This is why you'll see two-dollar bills with corners missing all over the country.

Acorn Lore

Acorns are magical. The squirrel in the movie *Ice Age* will tell you so. This little nut has been used as a charm for so many centuries, that you probably don't know why your grandmother crochets or wood-carves little figures of acorns to place around the house.

From Great Britain to Scandinavia, acorns are thought to bring youth and luck. If a woman carries one in her pocket, it is believed she will stay younger and healthier for longer.

There is a story from Norse mythology that states that Thor hid under an oak tree while seeking shelter from thunder. This is the reason the oak is considered *his* tree. Which brings us back to questions about grandma's little charms. Well, people would place acorns on a windowsill or front doorframe, as tribute to Thor and to ask for protection against thunder and lightning. In addition to grandma's charms, you've probably noticed that on Venetian window blinds, there are little acorn-shaped spheres at the ends of the cords that adjust the blinds. This superstition is responsible for those! One last bit—the acorn is thought to resemble the male organ (shocker), ensuring the family line would continue with this little charm hanging around.

The Portrait-Teller

I recently attended the opening night of a local artist's exhibition at a gallery, and, while browsing the exotic paintings, stopped short when a large piece fell. Shortly after the hubbub of the artist and his entourage ended, and the painting was saved, I wondered about the instinctual fear I had when it fell from the wall. Why I was struck with a feeling doom? Was it the mysterious complimentary drink? The heat of the lights?

As history will tell us, I'm not the only one who has had this feeling. Luckily, this painting was not a portrait of anyone. The superstition goes…if a portrait falls from a wall, it marks their impending death. Some people believe this only happens if the glass breaks.

There is a popular tale of an archbishop in England who walked into his study one day, and found his portrait lying on the floor. Seeing this may have terrified him, causing him to fall ill and quickly die. The same thing happened to The Duke of Buckingham during King Charles I's reign. He walked into his study, saw his portrait lying flat on the floor, and died shortly afterwards. (By the way, who keeps a portrait of *themselves* in their own study?) Awkward.

The origin of this superstition is similar to that of shoes. Portraits were believed to carry the essence of their subjects, and, for this reason, their fates were intertwined. Nowadays, this is still present in some cultures. Though it often applies to any painting. So, even if it is a painting of a fruit or a landscape, the omen could apply to whoever is in the house or in closest proximity to the fallen painting.

Now that I know this, I'm starting to worry. The painting at that gallery wasn't a portrait, but, it fell exactly when I passed it. Strange. I wonder…is that an omen for me? Now I'm nervous. Oh no. I think I feel a tickle in my throat…

POPULAR SUPERSTITIONS TODAY

Blessing the Sneeze

Like so many superstitions, why we say "bless you" after someone sneezes isn't clear. A popular theory is that your soul leaves your body when you sneeze, and blessing someone provides them protection from evil spirits taking the place of their loosey goosey soul. Versions of this blessing are said in over seventy languages—definitely a "contagious" superstition!

Knock on Wood

In an early nineteenth-century game of tag, if a child touched the wood of a tree, they would be "safe" from being caught. This is most likely originates from the "touch wood" superstition, where we knock or touch wood when we say something we don't want to happen (to avoid tempting fate).

Spilling the Salt

Originally, if salt was spilled in your direction, you would get bad luck (not whoever spilled it). It is only in more modern times that the person who spilled the salt would get bad luck. One of the most likely connection (there are many) is that Judas overturned the salt at the last supper, and throwing it over your shoulder would prevent the devil from whispering in your left ear (the weakest ear). Or, one could draw a cross in the salt. Salt has been considered a valuable commodity throughout history, almost like money, and is often connected to prosperity. After all, it is where we get the word "salary" from (*salarium* in Latin). "Wasting" it could be seen as inviting tragedy upon yourself and your family.

Walking Under a Ladder

This is a murky one. Opinions on how this superstition originated differ depending on who you ask. Some consider walking underneath a ladder to be sacrilegious, since a ladder leaning against a wall makes a triangle (i.e. with three points like Holy Trinity). Others say that it comes from having condemned individuals walk up a ladder to reach the gallows. And some even take a practical standpoint: that something could fall on you! Knowing the inconvenience of paint and plaster on one's head— this gets my vote.

We Prescribed That?

MEDICAL CURES, QUACKS, AND CRAZINESS

*"A doctor is nothing more than consolation
for the spirit."*

—Gaius Petronius Arbiter

Tell Me about Your Medical History

Where do we go when we're in pain…feeling helpless, and desperately seeking relief? A shrink might fit the bill. Or a physician, if it's physical. But, if you could get both, even better. In days of yore, before doctoring became the respectable profession it is now, doctors *were* a bit of both. And the quacks out there knew this.

When our ancestors were hit with diseases, painful accidents, or if there was simply something they wished for—like pregnancy or eternal youth—doctors gave promises…they gave hope. That is why this chapter's epigraph from Gaius Petronius Arbiter rings so true. "A doctor is nothing more than consolation for the spirit."

Did a physician treating a poor soul suffering from a debilitating illness really believe sticking a tube up his butt, and blowing tobacco smoke into it, would do the trick? Of course they did. They also believed drilling a hole into your skull might cure your depression.

While there are, of course, many cures that ancient doctors got right, why not instead focus on the ones they got shamefully wrong? Or simply examine the crazy stories, head-scratching remedies, and interesting discoveries? Our medical history is as interesting and inventive as we are, and will make you think of how much (and how little!) things have really changed. Even today, there are doctors, pharmaceutical companies, and quacky-ish sources pushing pills and remedies upon us like it was 1399. Promises.

Whether it comes in the form of tobacco enemas or other questionable practices, there will always be someone trying to blow smoke up your butt, to promise you *something*, to give you hope. It's up to you to decide if you're letting that tube down there.

Freshly Dead and Ready for Business

There are many befuddling medical cures from our past, but usually there is some sort of logic or dubious theory to be found that kind of makes sense if you squint and look sideways. However, logic escapes me where corpse medicine is concerned, and I'm baffled at how it went on for so long. Physicians have used corpses for a variety of "medical cures," and even cosmetic purposes since ancient Greek and Roman times.

From healing warts to staying young, all parts of our human bodies have been believed to contain a certain purpose. You will find records upon records of prescriptions from the past that include human ingredients—from hair, body fat, and urine, to breast milk, stool, and menstrual blood. Some of the ingredients, however, like fat and bone, can only be retrieved when the human donor is not alive to object. You could make a pretty penny off the dearly-departed.

The hottest commodities for healing were just-dead criminals. The theory for this most likely comes from Flemish scientist and physician Jan Baptiste van Helmont, who believed the life force of the body lingered after death. If the deceased had a particularly violent death, it would be even stronger. Let's explore some ways freshly dead bodies (and anciently dead mummy bodies) were used to "cure."

Hangman's Salve

What is hangman's salve, and why does it sound like something you don't want to try? Well, I won't leave you hanging too long. Hangman's salve is just another name for the fat of freshly executed criminals. Also known as "man's grease" and "poor sinner's fat." It was used for a host of cures for ailments ranging from gout to curing open wounds.

The fat would be sold to apothecaries, but was also claimed by executioners. It was not uncommon in the Netherlands for an executioner to use the human fat as a salve for the wounds of other prisoners that had just been tortured. It was quite the hot commodity in the past, and continued to be used until the *early nineteenth century*. How is this possible? Well, as time went on, the ingredient was advertised less. You could have been buying it in a cosmetic product, and simply not have known.

So, how exactly do you…you know…*get* the fat off our bodies? Sixteenth-century physician, Andreas Vesalius, recommended extracting bones and cartilage from a cadaver by boiling the body, and saving the human fat that drifted to the water's surface for its healing properties.

There are some theories on how this medical remedy came about, the most likely origins have to do with superstition. There is an ancient belief that the fat of saints and martyrs contained miraculous healing powers. Also, witches were known to consume narcotic herbs mixed with the fat of children on Witches' Sabbath, because they believed it contained the vitality of the young person who had passed. It wouldn't take long for beliefs of this nature to evolve into van Helmont's theory. Folklore is the cause of many practices from both past and present.

Despite the cringe-worthiness of the belief itself, the use of human fat as a healing agent is not based *entirely* on superstition. Modern medicine has revealed that adipose tissue (i.e. fat) is highly "angiogenic," meaning, it promotes the growth of new blood vessels from preexisting ones. So, those seeing results led others to believe it was effective without asking too many questions.

According to the *American Journal of Pharmacy and the Sciences*, a popular author in the seventeenth century told the story of a soldier who had been stabbed by a spear, but managed to recover completely by taking "a mixture of human fat, the blood of a he-goat, and Benedict water in beer." And for any cramps that occurred, an ointment "consisting of human fat, dog's fat, and the marrow of a horse-bone." All I have to say is…why does the goat have to be a he?

But for real. How human fat cures went on for millennia has me as stumped as the freshly beheaded.

> *"If doctors were aware of the power of this substance, no body would be left on the [gallows] for more than three days."*

—Paracelsus, Swiss physician and alchemist

The King's Drops

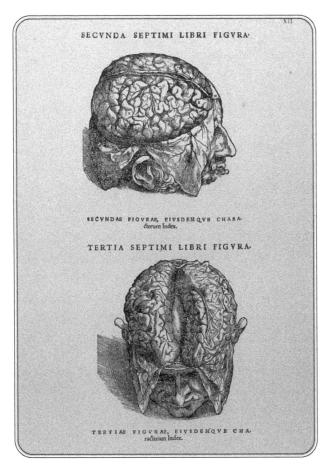

This curious seventeenth-century remedy gets its name from its most notable user: Charles II of England. Also known as Goddard's Drops, The King's Drops was a mixture of powdered human skull distilled in alcohol. Charles purchased the recipe from the physician, Johnathan Goddard, for about six thousand pounds, and often made it himself in his personal laboratory. The tincture was used to cure plights such as epilepsy, fainting, convulsions, lethargy, mental diseases, and to restore life to those on the brink of death.

To make this macabre eau de skull cocktail, all you need is:

☞ The spirit of hartshorn (a.k.a. ammonia)
☞ Powdered skull of a person recently hung
☞ A touch of dried viper

Thomas Willis, a seventeenth-century neurologist, brewed a variation of this spirit that contained chocolate. You know the saying, "a spoonful of sugar." This recipe was not the first to include skull. Charles II's grandfather, James I, was once prescribed it, but was known not to like it; a physician noted, "the king hates eating human bodies, [so] an ox's head can be substituted in his case."

The King's Drops became fashionable after Charles began using them. But after Charles II employed the drops on his death bed and, well, died anyway, their reputation took a bit of a hit. Their use faded during the Victorian era. Their popularity may be connected with the theory of "like curing like." Conditions like epilepsy were (correctly) believed to be due to a head issue, so it was only logical that brains and skulls would be the cure.

You might also find someone drinking water or wine from a skull, or stuffing some skull moss (the fungus that grew on really old skulls) up their nose to cure nosebleeds. John French, a "Doctor of Physick" made another recommendation in his book *The Art of Distillation*.

> "Take the brains of a young man that has died a violent death, together with the membranes, arteries, veins, nerves, all the [pulp] of the back, and bruise these in a stone mortar until they become a kind of pap. Then put as much of the spirit of wine as will cover… Then digest it half a year in horse dung… A scruple or two of this essence taken in some specifical water once in a day is a most infallible medicine against the falling sickness."
>
> —"The Essence of Man's Brains" recipe

If you want confirmation that these were instructions to drink brains and flesh that had been marinated in horse shit for six months: yes. But don't worry. You were supposed to dilute it with some water, of course.

"I find the medicine worse than the malady."

—John Fletcher, Jacobean playwright

Vampire Medicine

Human blood was another popular curative often prescribed in the past. Physicians would advocate it for numerous ailments, from epilepsy to restoring vitality. Fifteenth-century Italian scholar, Marsilio Ficino, believed blood would not only cure, but was the elixir of life itself. Ficino held that the elderly could restore a bit of their youth by sucking the blood of a healthy, young person. Like an actual vampire.

"Suck, therefore, like leeches, an ounce or two from a scarcely opened vein of the left arm..."

If you had "difficulty digesting raw blood," he recommended, "let it first be cooked together with sugar; or let it be mixed with sugar and moderately distilled over hot water and then drunk." Add some hot sauce and celery, and you have a right Bloody Mary on your hands.

One other particularly disgusting method of consuming blood was preserved blood jam. A recipe from a Franciscan apothecary in 1679 recommends you take the blood from a person of "warm, moist temperament, such as those of a blotchy, red complexion and rather plump of build." So, if you see a Weasley walking around... Then you were supposed to "let it dry into a sticky mass." I'll let your imagination take over there. Next:

> "Place it upon a flat, smooth table of soft wood, and cut it into thin little slices, allowing its watery part to drip away. When it is no longer dripping, place it on a stove on the same table, and stir it to a batter with a knife… When it is absolutely dry, place it immediately in a very warm bronze mortar, and pound it, forcing it through a sieve of finest silk. When it has all been sieved, seal it in a glass jar. Renew it in the spring of every year."

These prescriptions are all from living persons, though, what about the corpse medicine we've been talking about? The belief in the powerful healing nature of blood originated thousands of years ago, during Etruscan times, but was more popularly noted during Roman times, when people would drink the blood of fallen gladiators. Just like human fat, blood was thought best when taken from someone healthy, preferably young and strong. Who better fit that description than a strong fighter? As the gladiator died, sick people would go forth, and collect their blood. Once gladiatorial combat was prohibited, around 400 CE, executed criminals replaced them as a blood source. Common folk who attended executions would wait with their cups and bowls in hand, and rush forward to collect the blood that poured from just-executed criminals on the scaffold. Get it while it's hot, right?

> *"We preserve our life with the death of others. In a dead thing insensate life remains which, when it is reunited with the stomachs of the living, regains sensitive and intellectual life."*
>
> —Leonardo da Vinci

Elixir of Mummy

We've used human fat, fresh off the chopping block, the blood of both healthy and of freshly dead people, human skulls, and next on the menu are *really* old dead bodies—mummies.

Just like skulls, you wouldn't just eat a mummy like you were taking a bite off a Medieval festival turkey leg. You had to cut little bits off, and usually, powder it. The following recipe is physician John French's for "Elixir of Mummy" to cure "all infections."

> Take of mummy (viz., of man's flesh hardened), cut small, four ounces, spirit of wine…ten ounces, and put them into a glazed vessel (three parts of four being empty) which set in horse dung to digest for the space of a month.

More horse dung, you ask? What, you thought filet of mummy was the worst part of the recipe?

> Then take it out and express it, and let the expression
> be circulated a month. Then let it run through manica
> hippocratis [a filter bag], and then evaporate the spirit until
> that which remains in the bottom be like an oil which is the
> true elixir of mummy.

A month to marinate in horse dung, and another month for it to breathe. You must have patience for these recipes. It allows time to reflect on what you're about to do, and to psyche yourself up for it. But, if he's correct, all infections will be cured with this elixir. So it will all be worth the wait. French also states the mummy elixir is "very balsamical"—the meaning of which, I've yet to discover. Here's to hoping it has nothing to do with salads.

Put Some VapoRub on It

If you've ever seen the movie *My Big Fat Greek Wedding,* you will understand that some cultures have holy grail cure-alls. In that movie, it's Windex. From boils to pimples, the Greek dad tells his family to "put some Windex on it" for it to go away. In most Hispanic cultures, it's Vicks VapoRub. More commonly called *El Vickisito* (little Vicks), *El Bix*, *El Bic*, *Bibaporrú*, Eau De ViVapoRu, and *Vivaporú*.

Vivaporú (pronounced vee-vah-poh-roo) has become an iconic staple in Latin culture, with powers bordering on the supernatural. Mexican poet, José Olivarez, even wrote a poem about this little bottle of healing. Here is a short preview from this talented poet:

> miss a day of church? put some vaporub on your forehead &
> watch forgiveness flush your cheeks. put some vaporub on our
> bank account and watch the bill collectors stop calling. when
> i forget a word in Spanish? take a teaspoon of vaporub under
> the tongue.

Abuelas (grandmas) everywhere prescribe this little blue bottle for a host of ailments, most that have nothing to do with a cold. Mosquito bite? Vivaporú. Bad karma? Vivaporú. I can speak to this, being Hispanic myself. A few of the other common symptoms it has been used to treat include breakouts, nausea, headache, earache, stretch marks, sore muscles, and athlete's foot. Basically, when in doubt…put some Vivaporú on it!

Laugh Your Gas Off

"I felt like the sound of a harp."

Nitrous oxide is the fancy term for one of the greatest medical discoveries ever made—laughing gas. I was fortunate (ish?) to need a minor surgery where I was given nitrous instead of anesthesia, and wow—what an experience it was. It was one of the best feelings of my life. You remain mostly conscious while under nitrous, and I vaguely remember quoting *Hamlet* from memory, while a nurse played classical music on her phone, and I hummed along, as if in a dream. Don't judge. If you are unfamiliar with its effects, inhaling nitrous causes feelings of euphoria, and complete calm. It often causes hysterical giggling too, which is where its name comes from. Basically, just imagine floating peacefully in heaven, without a care in the world, and everything is funny.

The gas was first discovered in 1772 by English chemist, Joseph Priestley, but its potential remained undiscovered for decades. At the turn of the century, this magical compound's potential for pain relief was discovered by English physician, Thomas Beddoes, and English chemist, inventor, and baron, Sir Humphry Davy. Bless them. On an aside, Davy also discovered chlorine, iodine, and made dozens of other contributions to science and medicine. Smart baron.

Davy inhaled nitrous in the lab one day, and discovered bliss. Davy and Beddoes wanted to see how others reacted to the gas, so they threw wild parties, which Davy deemed "experiments," where he pumped his guests full of nitrous, and recorded their reactions. He took notes on over thirty people's experiences—all reported feeling intense joy. Some said they felt weightless, others, like the sound of a harp, with wild thoughts bursting from their mind. Poet Samuel Coleridge described a state of peaceful ecstasy, "like returning from a walk in the snow into a warm room."

These parties began popping up throughout the US and England in the first half of the 1800s. They were called "ether frolics," and were especially popular among chemistry and medical students. Though exquisitely fun, however, the parties held a greater purpose of *discovery* for Davy. The numbing effects of nitrous were noted, so, it started to be used during surgeries, as an early anesthesia, and for pain relief. The recreational use of nitrous eventually faded away, and after Davy discovered nitrous' addictive nature by becoming addicted himself, he swore it off for personal use, and only continued objective research. This happy little gas is now regulated, and should only be experienced in medical situations. But, if you happen to be throwing a wild, illegal ether frolic—I'll be expecting an invite!

Crapulence Begone!

Crapulence: the state of being intoxicated; a state of sickness caused by excessive drinking.

If any word best describes the feeling of a hangover, it's definitely *crapulence*. There are very few experiences worse than a hangover. You just feel like crap. But, while uncomfortable, they're also unavoidable (what are you going to do, just never drink)? Pha! Here are some cures we've cooked up in the past to deal with these next-day monsters.

Pokhmel'e

In 1635, German scholar Adam Olearius took a journey through Russia, and recorded an account of what he saw, and learned on his travels there. One of his chief observations was that the Russians loved to drink. "None of them anywhere, anytime, or under any circumstance lets pass any opportunity to have a draught or a drinking bout," he noted. How did they deal with the predictable and uncomfortable after-effects? Such professional drinkers had a tried and true recipe called *pokhmel'e*. It translates to "hangover" or "after being drunk."

To make this traditional recipe, here's what you do:

- ☞ Cut cold, baked lamb into small, thin strips
- ☞ Mix with peppers and cucumber (i.e. pickles), cut similarly
- ☞ Pour this over a mixture of equal parts vinegar and cucumber juice

Enjoy by eating with a spoon! Afterwards, Olearuis notes, "a drink tastes good again," You'll be ready to start all over.

Though probably very sour, there was steady logic behind this seemingly strange combination of foods. The lamb provides energy-giving protein. Pepper releases hydrochloric acid in the stomach, easing queasiness. The brine (rassol) of the pickles was crucial, due to the salt content, the electrolytes of which combat dehydration from drinking too much alcohol. Also, the malolactic fermentation of traditional Russian pickle-making would create what we now know as probiotics, which stimulate healthy bacteria in the gut.

The wisdom behind this medieval recipe has carried over today in the popularity of pickle juice. If you're into American football, you'll probably know that in 2000, players from the Philadelphia Eagles football team drank pickle juice before their game against the Dallas Cowboys. As a result, none of the Eagles players suffered from the muscle cramps that plagued the Cowboys. The Eagles won the game. Also, if you're at a bar, you can ask for something called The Pickleback, which is a shot of whiskey, followed by a shot of pickle juice. You can thank the Russians later!

> *"The vine bears three kinds of grapes: the first of pleasure, the next of intoxication, and the third of disgust."*
>
> —Anacharsis, sixth century BCE

Mesopotamian Stewage

Another interesting recipe from the past comes from ancient Mesopotamia. In 5000 BCE, a physician recommended whipping up the following stew:

> "If a man has taken strong wine and his head is affected… take licorice, beans, oleander, [with] oil and wine…in the morning before sunrise, and before anyone has kissed him, let him take it, and he will recover."

Before anyone has kissed him. That fast huh?

Licorice and wine are naturally sweet, beans are usually savory, but aside from the queasy clash of flavors, this cure might not be as repulsive as many others—except for the fact that oleander is a toxic plant. It might have worked by inducing vomiting, but too much and it would have been fatal. I think I'd rather take the headache to death.

> *"If an evening of wine does you in, more the next morning will be medicine."*
>
> —Medical School of Salerno

Cabbage Patch Cures: Hangover's Nemesis

The word *cabbage* does not suggest anything intimidating. In fact, it's kind of a silly word if you say it a few times in a row. Try it. Try it again. You get me? But, it's a fact that ancient Greeks and Romans considered cabbage plants the natural enemies of grapevines. They believed that even planting cabbage near a vine would cause the delicate vine to wither away.

This may be why the ancients thought cabbage would be so effective as a hangover cure! Too much wine in your system? It will run right out of you at the appearance of its sworn enemy, cabbage. Aristotle himself was known to swear by cabbage before and after drinking jaunts. Both Pliny the Elder, and Cato offer no less than eighty-seven ailments the mighty cabbage can cure.

But the truth is that cabbage *is* good for you, just not because it's the nemesis of wine.

It contains the amino acid glutamine, as well as potassium, sulfur, chlorine, iodine, Vitamin C, B6, and tons more nutrients including fiber to help absorb the alcohol acetaldehyde in your system.

You could eat this low-key bully several ways, preferably before and after your alcoholic escapade:

☞ Raw, served with vinegar, and lots of olive oil

☞ Boiled with the same

☞ Russian style, with pickled cabbage water (predictable much?)

☞ Ukrainian style, with sauerkraut

☞ Boil the cabbage, and just drink the juice

Also, Galen the Greek recommended wrapping your head in cabbage leaves, though, I'm wagering this made anyone witnessing this strange spectacle feel better than it would make you feel.

"If anyone have drunk too much, if it be a man, the testicles should be washed with salt and vinegar, and if it be a woman, the breasts, also let them eat the leaf or the stalk or the juice of a cabbage with sugar."

—*The Canterbury Tales*

Curative Wreaths

Speaking of wrapping your head in stuff. If you knew *anything* about the proper way to throw a banquet in ancient Greece, you would make sure to have wreaths available to decorate your guests' heads, and prevent hangovers. It was believed the unique fragrances of these wreaths would protect the wearer from the consequences of hitting the wine too hard.

Recently discovered Greek and Roman texts reveal there were entire books dedicated to the healing powers of wreaths. Certain flowers, plants, and leaves have healing powers, and combining them in a particular way was a skilled art.

For example, it was thought the smell of roses or myrtle would prevent headaches and cool down your "bad humors." Roses were considered a powerful sedative; henna, sage, and saffron could lull you into a peaceful sleep, and let you wake, rested.

Also, twining the leaves of the Alexandrian laurel shrub to wear around your neck was recommended after a night of wild Roman festivities, like the legendary bacchanalias. If there were plants associated with a specific god, those would be used resourcefully as well. For example, ivy, laurel, and asphodel were all linked to the god Dionysus, and were commonly used for a wide variety of medicinal purposes.

The renowned physician Triphonus wrote that flowered wreaths were "not simply ornamental, but served to ward off drunkenness, migraines, and other maladies" Perhaps, modern day, flower-crowned Coachella festivalgoers are channeling ancient wisdom after all.

WE DID THAT?: THE VERY FIRST VACCINE

English physician Edward Jenner created the first vaccine in 1796. Smallpox, or the pox, killed nearly half a million people every year in eighteenth-century Europe. Its appearance was akin to leprosy, and caused great fear, as it was usually fatal. The key to beating smallpox once and for all came from a rather odd source: cows.

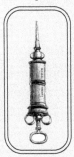

The *cowpox* virus was a more minor skin disease than smallpox, that cows and milkmaids developed, usually on their arms or legs. In his hypothesis that these two were connected, Jenner took the pus (I know, gross) from a lesion of a milkmaid infected with cowpox, and deposited the pus in the bloodstream of a young boy. He then exposed the boy to smallpox—*but nothing happened*. The boy didn't catch this highly infectious disease at all. This is why the word vaccine comes from the Latin word for cow: *vacca* (in Spanish, *vaca*).

A Holy Cure

We all have little remedies that make us feel better. Tummy ache? Some tea might be your go-to. Feeling a tickle in your throat? Probably VapoRub, and some hot chicken soup makes you feel better every time. But we all know that sometimes royals can be a bit...extra.

Whenever Ethiopian emperor Menelik II (1844–1913) felt the slightest bit ill, he was known to rip out and eat pages from the bible. God knows how this man reached the conclusion that bible paper cured all ills, but it must have worked for him at some point, because he did it for years. Maybe he just needed some fiber.

Things really turned the page for his little habit in 1913. After suffering a stroke, he went on a paper eating binge, and stuck to a diet consisting solely of the first and second book of Kings. He did survive the stroke, but ended up dying from an intestinal blockage...most likely from all the paper. *Too* much fiber, man.

In his defense, there *are* mentions in the bible to "eat" the word of God. But, perhaps if he had spent more time reading, and less time salivating, he might not have taken this piece of wisdom so literally. Here is one quote to note.

> *"Your words were found, and I ate them, and your words became to me a joy and the delight of my heart…"*
>
> —Jeremiah 15:16

If you were Menelik II, this means one thing: bon appétit.

Prescriptions that Quack

> *"Medicine sometimes grants health, sometimes destroys it."*
>
> —Ovid, *Tristia*

Leprosy No More

The following remedy will cure the pesky leprosy that is giving you such a bad rep. You no longer need face the embarrassment of having to wear a bell around your neck, and having everyone avoid you. But, I hope you're not scared of snakes. Especially fat, scary vipers. John French, well-known physician in the seventeenth century, and author of *The Art of Distillation*, recommends the following.

> Take of the best fat vipers, cut off their heads, take off their skins, and unbowel them. Then put them into the best canary sack [white fortified wine], four or six according to their

bigness into a gallon. Let them stand two or three months. Then draw off your wine as you drink it.

Some put them alive into the wine, and there suffocate them, and afterwards take them out, and cut off their heads, take off their skins, and unbowel them, and then put them into the same wine again, and do as before.

So, let me Spark Note this for you real quick. First, you find some vipers. Then you attempt to kill some vipers (without getting *yourself* killed). Then, you do some nasty stuff with their bodies, and let them stew in your white wine. Preferably, the one you've been saving for your anniversary.

Then you try and find some *more* vipers to capture, while at the same time trying not to get yourself killed in the process. Then you put those vipers *alive* into your wine, until they drown. You're going to have to wait awhile for this bit, since vipers can usually survive under water for over an hour. Then, you do some more nasty stuff to them. Then, repeat.

All in all, I think either the leprosy or snakes would have killed me by the time this wine was ready.

Virtuous Medical Dung

"…there is great virtue in dung."

In case you wanted to know how to make Water of Dung, you're covered. The following recipe, from our friend, John French has medicinal benefits, he claims, by making the ground fertile. He's actually got a good point there. Fertile ground allows food to grow. So, why use store-bought fertilizer anymore? Make your own dung tea by doing the following.

Ancient "still" apparatus used for distillation. The larger end
would be put under a flame.

Take of any dung as much as you please. While it is still fresh,
put it into a common cold still [pictured] and with a soft fire
distill it off. It will be best if the bottom of the still be set over
a vapor. If you would have it be stronger, cohobate the said
water over its feces several times; for we see there is great
virtue in dung. It makes ground fertile, and many sorts thereof
are very medicinal.

A Spirit to Irritate Your Spirits

You know exactly what you need on those days you *just can't?* Those
days when you more closely resemble a sloth than a productive
panda? Drink of the spirit of Aqua Magnanimitatis to lift you out of
your stupor. It's especially good if you must go to war, need courage,
want to pee a lot, or want to have lots of sex. Basically, it will be a
kick in the pants. Or, perhaps more appropriately, like having ants in
your pants.

You might know the main ingredient in this remedy— "pismire"—
by the more casual name of "piss ant" or "pissant," if you want to

sound French, and fancy. Basically, you're going to need a lot of these annoying little insects. Aqua Magnanimitatis will also cure deafness, or restore your vision, if you're getting a tad blind…but, I dare you to drop eau d'ant in your eyeballs.

> Take of pismires or ants (the biggest that have a sourish smell are the best) two handfuls, spirit of wine a gallon. Digest them in a glass vessel, close shut the space of a month in which time they will be dissolved into a liquor. Then distill them in balneum [a vessel for holding hot water] until all be dry. Then put the same quantity of ants as before. Digest and distill them in the said liquor as before. Do this three times, and then aromatize the spirit with some cinnamon.

> Note that upon the spirit will float an oil which must be separated.

> This spirit is of excellent use to stir up the animal spirit—in so much that John Casmire…did always drink of it when they went to fight, to increase magnanimity and courage which it did even to admiration.

> This spirit does also wonderfully irritate them that are slothful to venery [sexual indulgence].

> It also provokes urine even to admiration.

> It does also wonderfully irritate the spirits that are dulled and deeded with any cold distemper. This oil does the same effects, and indeed more powerfully.

> This oil does, besides what is spoken of the spirit, help deafness exceedingly, two or three drops being dropped into the ear, after it is well syringed, once in a day for a week together.

> It helps also the eyes that have any film growing on them, being now and then dropped into them.

John Casmire was a German prince in the sixteenth century, most of his battles would have been related to religious matters. So, if you're facing down a battle like he did, Aqua Magnanimitatis will get you pumped up during the battle pre-game.

I'm not sure why anyone would want to "provoke urine even to admiration"—perhaps a who-can-pee-farther contest between two mature men? Whatever the intention, this spirit was meant to be a sort of 5-Hour Energy drink with ants in it, to cure your slothful tendencies, and kick any lethargic feelings right out the door.

"Take your fee while the patient still feels ill."

—Common physician advice

Twenty-Seven Cures by Onion

They make you cry, they make your quesadilla taste amazing, and they make you think of "my heart is like an onion" similes. But, did you know that there are twenty-seven ways this layered veggie could cure you? According to Pliny the Elder anyway. Pliny was a multitalented Roman naturalist and philosopher in the first century. His life's work, *Natural History*, endeavors to capture tomes of ancient knowledge of the natural world. Regarding onions, here are some of the best of the twenty-seven cures he wrote about.

If you thought you hated the burning sensation in your eyes that comes with chopping onions, imagine rubbing the evil juice in your eyes. Pliny's first recommended use of the mighty onion is as a cure for those with vision problems. For "dimness of sight, the patient being made to smell at it till tears come into the eyes: it is still better even if the eyes are rubbed with the juice." By the end, you will be crying dramatically enough to win yourself an Oscar.

If you find yourself set upon by hounds from hell, and bitten, then Pliny recommends, "Fresh onions in vinegar, applied topically, or dried onions with wine and honey, are good for the bites of dogs, care being taken not to remove the bandage till the end of a couple of days. " Slathering yourself with onions several day's old sounds aromatic—just add some salt, and you'll be ready for the oven. He also writes that this same recipe for dog bites is good for curing skin damaged by being scratched and picked constantly.

Good news for those who've spent too many nights at their local brothel. Take the onion and, "Roasted in hot ashes, many persons have applied them topically, with barley meal, for defluxions [discharge] of the eyes and ulcerations of the genitals." Warning: it won't make you smell any better after your nighttime escapade.

There is apparently something about onions and honey that makes the combination prime for healing. He recommends it highly for snake bites, and any other wounds caused by animals, such as scorpion bites. Also, if you add some breast milk—I know—he claims, it can cure ear infections; or, if your ears are ringing, or you're going slightly deaf, just drop some down your ear canal "with goose-grease or honey."

Additional onion remedies include soothing digestion, acting as suppositories for the bowels, curing dropsy (fluid retention and swelling), quinsy (an inflammation of the tonsils), and "dispelling lethargy." And, my personal favorite: "In cases where persons have been suddenly struck dumb, it has been administered to them to drink, mixed with water." Two other ailments it cures are toothache and mouth ulcers—the juice of the onion is gargled in the mouth. Ooh…Listerine vs. onion juice mouthwash. Who would win? Ready, set, gargle.

Milk Transfusions

The history of blood transfusions is long and controversial. The first successful one was performed as early as the seventeenth century by physician Richard Lower. However, many of the cases started, and ended grimly, with a great deal of animal abuse. (Consider yourself warned.) Animals were the first test patients for transfusions, particularly dogs and lambs. Then, humans. Most outcomes ended up killing the donor, however, and the practice was condemned by Royal Society, the French government, and even the Vatican.

There were simply too many difficulties and dangers. The blood would often coagulate, patients died even after their lives had been saved, and donors would often die as well. Getting past these drawbacks seemed impossible. But by mid-nineteenth century, physicians were willing to try anything. Their next brilliant idea? Transfusions using a blood replacement. The replacement? Milk.

The first experiment happened in 1854, by Drs. James Bovell and Edwin Hodder. Their theory was that the oily and fatty particles in milk could be converted into "white corpuscles" or white blood cells. (Hey, milk is white, innit?) They injected forty-year-old patient zero with twelve-ounces of cow's milk. Surprisingly, he seemed to react well. So did the next patient. The next five times, however, the patients all died.

Despite the negative outcomes, however, the belief that milk was an effective substitute continued to be tested. Cow milk was mainly used, but then, goat milk, and eventually, human milk, to see if that was more compatible. The first patient stopped breathing within a few moments after human milk was introduced to her bloodstream. Thankfully, this practice wasn't milked much longer; it was disproven around 1884. By the turn of the century, in 1901, blood types were finally discovered, putting an end to milk transfusions once and for all.

> ### *"I am dying from the treatment of too many physicians."*
> ### —Alexander the Great

A BAD CASE OF THE SNEEZIES

Could you imagine sneezing once a minute for over two months straight? How about every few seconds? In 1966, seventeen-year-old June Clark from Miami lived this terrifying scenario. Somehow, after she had surgical procedure on her kidneys, her sneezing began out of the blue and didn't stop.

Her doctors were completely baffled and tried all different types of treatment, from hypnosis to infrared exposure. The only time she got some peace was while sleeping, and to do this she usually had to take drugs. Finally, the doctors tried electric therapy—shocking her every time she sneezed—and it worked!

Getting Preggy with It

Trying to get pregnant (or *not*) is a struggle most couples have dealt with since the dawn of our species. Without the perks of modern medicine, for centuries, physicians and midwives have had to make do with trial and error. For those who were desperate to get pregnant (not get pregnant), and willing to try anything, countless tricks and concoctions were prescribed to give eager couples their desire. Or at least raise their hopes for it. But hey, don't go trying these at home.

Grow a Pair

Following the infamous and ancient theory of "like cures like," we'll now cure a man's infertility with the same thing that is apparently causing it: his testicles.

In the Roaring Twenties, Russian-born physician Serge Voronoff had a wild theory. Since he believed lower hormonal activity happened as you aged, perhaps boosting hormone production could stop aging (and thus infertility). To test out his theory, he performed some self-experimentation, where he injected the ground testicles of dogs and guinea pigs into his own testicles. Nothing exactly happened, but for some reason, he believed the experiment paid off. My mother always told me men believed what they wanted to, and there was stopping them.

He soon began offering his services, but with small "slithers" of baboon testicles (because you can't exactly transplant full-sized baboon testicles into yours, sorry). The placebo effect was dominant, and the practice took off, but shriveled up after a few years. In the following century, this fad was taken up by "Doctor" John Romulus Brinkley. Make no mistake, Brinkley had fewer medical qualifications than Dr. Evil. No, his degree came from Eclectic Medical University in Kansas City (says it all really).

But, his ad—leading with "Do you wish continue as a sexual flat tire?"—insisted that men could restore their virility with a new set of testicles joined to the patient's current pair. From which animal would you procure the testicles this time, you ask? Goats.

An embarrassing number of men bought into this quacky fertility cure. What became of the men who were injured or impaired from being operated on by someone who probably never dissected a frog? Within a decade, unsurprisingly, his popularity faded, and he went bankrupt from numerous lawsuits.

On the other hand—and ironically—male animal nuts were prescribed in the past to *prevent* pregnancy too. Trota of Salerno, one of the few female physicians in the twelfth century, had a pretty savage prescription for keeping pregnancy at bay.

She recommended cutting off the testicles of a male weasel, and releasing it back into the wild. Then, wrapping the testicles in goose skin, and wearing them around your neck. I definitely think having a shriveled pair of nuts around your neck would make the guys give you a wide berth, and prevent any activities that remotely led to pregnancy. An effective contraceptive indeed! If these were human male testicles (preferably of your ex), then I would say this was less of a cruel contraceptive, and more of a power move.

Fertility Theme Park

In the late 1700s, electricity was starting to have a strong current in the medical world (sorry). Used for a variety of "treatments"—from helping flush out toxins, to reviving dead people—the plight of infertility didn't escape its reach either.

Another "doctor" named James Graham convinced his wealthy patrons to support many of his crazy endeavors. He went on to become one of the most notorious quacks of the eighteenth century. One of his most cray-cray experiments was the Temple of Health and Hymen. I think the name says it all, and I don't need to continue. I feel I can stop here, right? *That name.*

Anyways, the Temple of Health and Hymen opened in London in 1780, and, in essence, was a fertility theme park. It was filled with women dressed as "goddesses," wearing as little clothing as possible, who recited verses to the god Apollo. But, the main attraction was Graham's electro-magnetic, musical "Grand State Celestial Bed." The whole purpose of the bed was to provide baby-making vibes by "gently pervading the whole system with a copious tide of that celestial fire."

There was even a motel-like service available, with the option of a *private* Celestial Bed. It was twelve feet long, and nine feet wide, balanced on dozens of pillars of colored glass, and decorated with large crimson tassels. Sweet perfumes were blown onto the bed, while get-it-on music played in the background. For only fifty pounds, couples could use the bed, and were guaranteed "immediate conception." A hefty promise. You'll be shocked to learn, he went bankrupt only a few years later.

Croikey Contraceptives

You'll be thanking heavens for your IUD in a moment. In ancient Egypt, a common form of birth control was none other than crocodile dung. The dung was dried into little pebbles, and inserted into the vagina, where it was softened by the heat of female body temperature, and formed a blockage for you-know-what. In India, the women were known to use elephant dung instead. You gotta use what you have… Now, all you have to do is explain to your man why things are a little stank down there.

The practice of putting weird ingredients *up there* was very common in ancient times. A few other contraceptive ingredients were ginger, tobacco juice, tree sap, olive oil, ghee, lemon juice, lemon halves, cotton, wool, and sea sponges. Basically, your entire pantry and bathroom drawer. Stuff it all up there. Hey, without the pill we had to get inventive, didn't we?

Some ingredients had *some* basis in reason, for example, we know now that lemon and acacia juice can act as spermicides. But, many others, specifically, animal droppings, simply made one smelly.

Is He All Dead? Or Mostly Dead?

In the wise words of Billy Crystal's character, Miracle Max, in *The Princess Bride*, "If he's mostly dead, I can save him; if he's all dead—there's only one thing you can do. Go through his clothes and look for loose change."

So, in the past, how did we know someone was all dead? That they had really and truly crossed over to the other side? That they weren't just in a temporary state of mostly deadness, and would reawaken in a little while? In the seventeenth and eighteenth centuries, there was general public panic of being accidentally buried alive (called taphophobia by the way). After several stories circulated of this happening, it's no wonder.

In 1740, the French anatomist Jacques Bénigne Winslow wrote that, "The onset of putrification was the only reliable indicator that the subject had died." Scary, innit? What could that say about the people who were buried before their bodies started to decompose? Thankfully Winslow created some precautionary measures to determine all deadness.

> "The individual's nostrils are to be irritated by introducing sternutaries, errhines [tools that could make you sneeze], juices of onions, garlic and horseradish... The gums are to be rubbed with garlic, and the skin stimulated by the liberal application of whips and nettles [a really itchy plant]. The intestines can be irritated by the most acrid enemas, the limbs agitated through violent pulling, and the ears shocked by hideous Shrieks and excessive Noises. Vinegar and salt should be poured in the corpse's mouth and where they cannot be had, it is customary to pour warm Urine into it, which has been observed to produce happy Effects."

When all else failed, you could cut slits in the bottom of their feet, thrust needles under their nails, and even putting a hot poker up their anus (getting kinky eh?).

Precoffinary Measures

In response to the horror stories of people being buried alive, inventors got innovative and crafted special coffins that let the person inside signal for help if they happened to, you know, *not* actually be dead. One such inventor, John Krichbaum, patented his very practically named "Device for Indicating Life in Buried Persons" in December, 1882. In case they were "under doubt of being in a trance," there would be a T-shaped pipe inside the coffin itself, and the person's hands would rest on either end of the T. Leading out of the pipe, would be a tube that reached the ground overhead. If the person was alive, when they woke up, their hands would disrupt the T-pipe, since that's where their hands are placed. By way of a cross-pin, and a few other complicated mechanisms, it would show above, on the invention's display, that the pipe had been disturbed. If the person should "make any more violent motion," it would then *turn*. This would open up the tube, so that air from above could enter, until help arrived. To keep rain or water from entering the tube over time, the tube and display could be covered by glass, so people could still monitor the status.

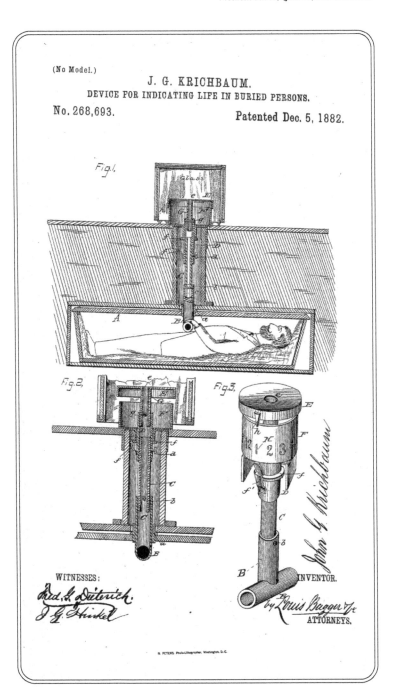

(No Model.)

J. G. KRICHBAUM.
DEVICE FOR INDICATING LIFE IN BURIED PERSONS.
No. 268,693.   Patented Dec. 5, 1882.

Fig.1.

Fig.2.   Fig.3.

WITNESSES: INVENTOR.
                              John G. Krichbaum
                              by Louis Bagger & Jr.
                              ATTORNEYS.

N. PETERS, Photo-Lithographer, Washington, D.C.

This is just one crafty coffin that added some actual life insurance. Another one, invented in 1868, used a bell and a ladder. Above the ground, there was a bell with a rope attached to it, and leading down into the coffin, a rope would be tied around the person's hand. If there were any movement, people would be alerted immediately by the bells. Hopefully, someone would be around to hear them. Not many just stroll around graveyards in their free time, unless they're tombstone tourists (which is a macabre-yet-cool hobby, by the way). Still, it was a cool invention for this very real medical phobia. And speaking of cool inventions… It looks like it's time to leave the world of medicine, and explore the world of wacky inventions aimed to please us, and (for some) make us cackle in glee…

We Invented That?

SURPRISING AND WACKY INVENTIONS

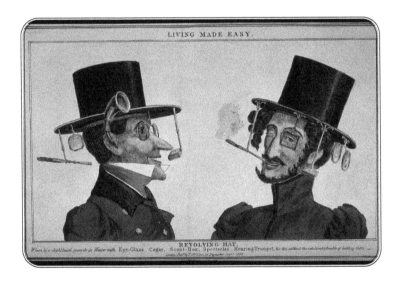

"We often find what will do by finding out what will not do; and probably he who never made a mistake never made a discovery."

—Samuel Smile, *Self Help*, 1859

The Pioneers of Invention

In this chapter, you'll discover how true it is that there are no limits to our imagination. If we can dream it, we can achieve it. If we can imagine it, we can invent it. If someone can picture a top hat that carries our cigarette, music, glasses, and perfume all at once—it can be created. If someone envisions a surfing wheel for humans in the same style of a hamster wheel, it can be invented. Or at the least, it can be patented!

Some inventions, though patented, never see the light of day. Others are the early models for many conveniences we enjoy today. Did you know the treadmill was originally invented as a torture device? Well, if you've ever used one, I'm sure you guessed this was its purpose all along. Did you know roller skates originally resembled small bicycles for your feet? All inventions have their embarrassing braces-and-pimples stage.

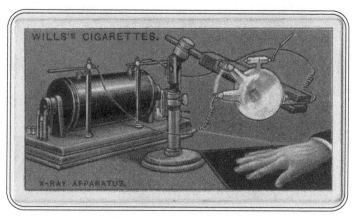

An etching of an early x-ray machine, which was discovered by accident in 1895 by Wilhelm Conrad Röntgen.

The ingenuity of humans is endless, and our minds continue to break the boundaries of logic today. A keyboard and mouse installed on your jeans for people too lazy to carry theirs around? Yes. Scissors specifically designed to cut and serve pizza? Yes. Our brilliance has not faded with the years. But, for a moment, let's look at our past strokes of genius.

The Mousetrap Pistol

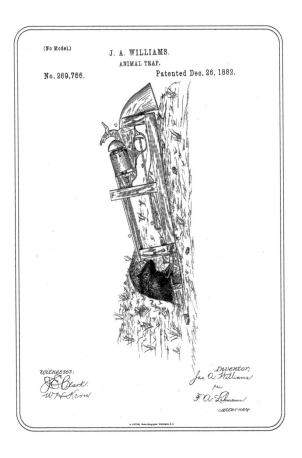

In 1882, the Texan inventor James Williams took out a patent on an invention he humbly titled "Animal Trap." This trap's purpose was gleefully stated, "to provide a means by which animals which burrow in the ground can be destroyed"—with a pistol. In the mechanics of the trap, Williams used a simple, but delicately arranged system that relied on the pressure of the mouse (much like today's traps), to cause the shot. Once the mouse stepped on the board or "treadle," a lever was forced into small pole that put pressure on the trigger. In a nutshell, it was a mousetrap that joined the mob.

You might be wondering where exactly he got this idea. Well, there *was* a similar invention that existed at that time, but was used as a burglar alarm, rigged to a front door or a window. Williams make it clear his trap could also be used for this purpose, though the mechanics of his alarm were very different (i.e. "I didn't steal their idea").

While his invention might be *kind of an aggressive* way to handle a mouse problem, Williams stated that it had an added benefit of providing, well, the *alarm*. It gave notice that the mouse was caught (destroyed, obliterated, same thing), and that the trap had to be reset. Thankfully, about a decade later, the mousetrap we know today was invented. Phew. I would hate to have bumped into a mouse trap like this by accident—I don't think my foot would have recovered.

THE FIRST PATENT

The very first US patent was granted to Philadelphia man Samuel Hopkins, in 1790, by (drum roll) President George Washington himself. The patent was for his unique "potash" recipe—an ingredient used in fertilizer. Not the most exciting invention, we can admit. Though it definitely fertilized the way to the millions of patents we have today. (Sorry.)

"Our inventions mirror our secret wishes."

—Lawrence Durrell

The Unsinkable Safe

This bit is less about a crazy invention, and more about a crazy *inventor*—though aren't they all that way? In 1915, two Italian friends, Menotti Nanni, and Giuseppe Bertolini, invented the unsinkable safe.

Being just a few years after the sinking of the *Titanic*, I'd wager that "unsinkable" wasn't a good PR term. But, it's possible these two inventors were inspired by this very tragedy, which doubtless caused many to lose their belongings to the bottom of the sea.

With this in mind, these two Italian inventors crafted a large, pill-shaped vault made of material "solid as concrete yet light as cork," embedded within its casing to make it float, as well as an airtight door to prevent leakage. Menotti Nanni claimed it was "absolutely burglar and fire-proof and unsinkable besides." With their purchase, customers were given a key, tailored specifically to them, to wear on their wrist. That way, if the ship sank, only they would be able to open their safe. Alternately (and morbidly), if the passenger drowned, the key on their wrist would serve as a means of identifying them.

To get to the crazy part, on one sunny day in New York City, 1915, Nanni decided to put the invention to the test. Just off the harbor at Battery Park, Nanni locked himself inside the safe and, with the help of friends, was dropped into the water to sink. And sink he did. But then, after one tension-filled minute, Nanni's safe slowly and victoriously emerged to the surface.

Witnesses and collaborators gather in the boat that took Nanni into the harbor off Battery Park, NY.

In this photo you can see Nanni and Bertolini's safe slowly emerging.

A rowboat then paddled into the water to release him from his box of steel, and Nanni emerged, victorious. Amid the celebration and flag-waving that followed, this photo was captured. If you saw this photo without any context, it might look like he was in a mini-submarine. That's how accommodating the safe was for a full-grown adult. The image freezes Nanni and company in time, waving the American and Italian flags, and basking in their success after such a risky mission.

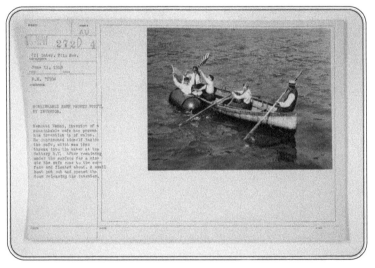

Nanni in the water, just having emerged to the surface, proving the success and value of his invention.

If we could take a moment to simply imagine the daring nerve it must have taken for him to lock himself in a pitch-black safe weighing three tons of steel, and to be dropped into a harbor, twenty to thirty feet deep—without knowing if he'd make it back up... That's one crazy inventor!

The Mean, Teeny Reading Machine

I'm an avid reader. I like big books, and I cannot lie. But, throughout my reading career I don't think I've ever said to myself, *I wish the font in this book was smaller.* But, it seems someone has!

In the early 1920s, Rear Admiral Bradley Fiske invented the Fisk Reading Machine, which many anticipated would be the "next big thing" for books. This handheld metal machine could contain a whole book, printed in teeny letters, on just a few cards. The cards would be inserted into the machine, which readers would hold up their eyes, and look through a magnifying glass in order to read. While I am getting a headache just thinking about it, there were indeed some benefits to this interesting invention:

☞ It's compact and easy to carry around.

☞ It takes almost no space to store your books.

☞ Has low printing costs, so it could be sold to publishers only four cents (and to customers for cheap!)

☞ Makes knowledge available to anyone: due to lower prices, even lower-income individuals can experience the pleasure of reading.

☞ It is environmentally sustainable, since it takes only a fraction of the paper that regular books take to produce.

☞ Eyeglasses and spectacles not required!

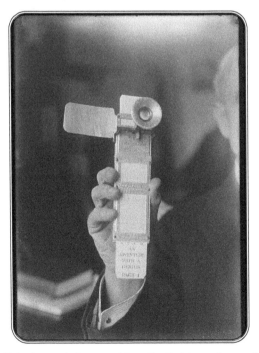

Fiske demonstrates a card from the first two volumes of Mark Twain's *Innocents Abroad*.

Despite all its benefits and all the attention it received, however, it never reached mass production. But it sparked a revolution in micro-media formats, such as microphotography, which has continued until today. If you wish to see an original prototype of this teeny reading machine, you can currently see it at the Rosenbach Museum and Library in Philadelphia, PA. And speaking of libraries…if you want to experience most of the benefits of this invention, just visiting your local library will do the trick!

The Light at the End of the Toilet

Getting up in the middle of the night to pee is a dangerous task—fraught with furniture corners that appear out of nowhere, waiting to stub bare toes, hard walls that are closer than they appear in the day, and a completely wide-open porcelain toilet bowl, that may, or may not, have the lid up. You have two choices: turn on the blazing light and squint in ocular agony, or fumble in the dangerous dark.

In inventor Brooke Pattee's more humble words, you are "faced with the unpleasant choice of using the bathroom with either too little light or with too much light." Pattee probably got sick of having to choose, because in 1993, she patented her toilet landing light. A hopeful beacon to full bladders everywhere. A lighthouse in the midnighty darkness. Stopping now.

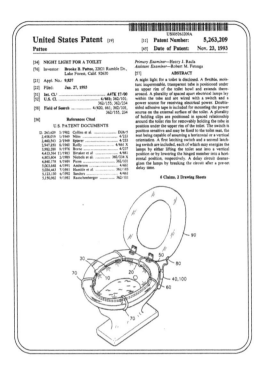

Her toilet light is made of a "flexible, moisture impermeable, transparent tube [and] positioned under an upper rim of the toilet bowl and extended around the toilet bowl." It was motion-activated, so that when approached, it lit up your chamber pot. Almost like a night light… There were other patents over the years, that sought to create something of this kind, but all failed, because she said they didn't fill the "need for a toilet night light that is easy to install, easy to use, and easy to clean." Pattee's did.

Her invention didn't quite make it big, however, but several other variations have been put on the market over the years, including a colorful one that makes your toilet bowl look like a really hip nightclub. I've already placed my order.

I Smell an Invention

Writers write things. Inventors invent things. But, every once in a while…inventors invent things that writers have written about. Or perhaps…*predicted*.

In fact, many of the most daring advancements were born from stories. Fictional tales created in order to shock, entertain, and, sometimes, warn the world. Think *1984*, *Brave New World*, or *Blade Runner*. Advances like cloning, artificial intelligence, and laboratory births—many of these possibilities were originally conceived of in fiction, and later brought to life by inventors. Life imitating art. Or— more appropriately—life inspired by art.

I mention this, because there is an invention that I personally believe was inspired by a scene in one of my favorite novels. In the dystopian book, *Brave New World*, by Aldous Huxley, the two main characters go out on a date to catch a "feely." That's the nickname for a movie where you can feel, smell, and taste all the sensations of the main characters. The smell of a city street, the wind on your face, even sexual touch. This novel was published in 1932.

Less than thirty years later, in 1960, osmologist Hans Laube and director Mike Todd Jr. invented Smell-O-Vision. It was an invention for movie theaters that released odors at certain times during the film—letting people actually smell what was going on. The coolest thing was that the scents would be integral to the plot and nuances of the story. The inventors had high hopes that it would become a phenomenon.

Unfortunately, the first, and only, film to ever use Smell-O-Vision was *Scent of Mystery* in 1960. It is a murder mystery based on the 1947 novel, *Ghost of a Chance,* by Kelley Roos. Throughout the two-hour movie, thirty different scents were pumped into the theater, prompted by the music soundtrack. The odors gave the viewers (smellers?) hints about plot, or simply let them experience other details, like what an entire casket filled with spilled wine smelled like. When the casket spilled, a potent perfume of grapes would be released. Some plot hints included a waft of pipe smoke, which gave a clue as to who the villain was.

The original experiment didn't work out as expected, mainly due to technical difficulties. Either the scents would get pumped at the wrong time, or they were hardly detectable, or way too strong. The film flopped quickly. But you have to admit, the Smell-O-Vision experience had some promise, even though it wasn't as scentsational as planned...

Deep Sea Dogs

If you have ever wished you could take your canine best friend everywhere (including deep sea diving), you are not alone. Florida native Dwayne Folsom took his furry lady, Shadow, with him *everywhere*. But when it came to taking her underwater, he was quite stuck. When he would go diving, she would jump off their boat, and try to follow his trail of bubbles. Queue the awws. He hated not being able to take her underwater with him, so he looked for a solution.

In 1997, he applied for a patent he named "Canine Scuba Diving Apparatus." He specifically modified a human scuba diving regulator to fit Shadow, and attached a spherical helmet to it, kind of like an astronaut's headgear. The opening of the helmet was lined with a skirt of water-resistant material, which both sealed the helmet, and also acted as a cushion for her neck. Also, Folsom installed an intercom system so he would be able to communicate with her.

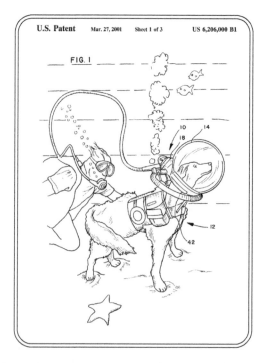

Since filing his original patent, there have been several modifications made to this device, but since then, Shadow was recorded to have at least thirty dives to her name, though, that number is likely much higher at the time of this writing. That is one ingenious inventor, and one adventurous dog!

The Aquarium Watch

Who knew checking the time on your watch could be such a bore? Add some excitement to this routine gesture with the Aquarium Watch, patented July 2002, by Harold Von Braunhut. This invention is exactly what it sounds like: a very small aquarium attached to a timepiece. The wearer can simultaneously tell time, while also enjoying teeny tiny aquatic life roaming around on your wrist.

The reason for Von Braunhut's invention is pure enjoyment. Having a fish tank full of creatures at home is lovely and all, but you can't exactly enjoy it while you are at school or otherwise away from home, right? So, instead of looking at your mundane, non-aquatic wristwatch, counting down the hours, impatiently wondering how much time is left before you can finally go home and enjoy your fish…why not carry your tank with you wherever you go? In Von Braunhut's own words:

> *"There is a need, therefore, for a means to allow fish lovers and the like to enjoy their aquatic friends 'round the clock,' so to speak."*

How does one get such small creatures into a dome roughly smaller than a golf ball? A marine life kit is provided with the product, which contains another one of his inventions called Amazing Sea Monkeys, a variant species of teeny brine shrimp. These come in ant-sized eggs and hatch shortly after contact with water. The aquarium itself is detachable, and comes with a plug, in order to add the marine life, feed it, and regulate the environment—just as you would with a normal fish tank.

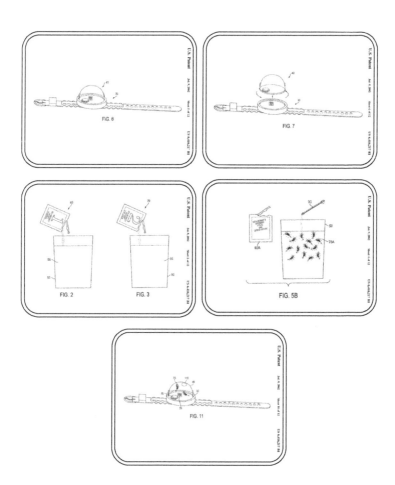

The Snake Collar

Of all the creatures to take for a walk around the block—a snake wouldn't be my first pick. But, I think anyone with four names on his birth certificate is bound to have a certain level of imagination, and that is indeed the case for Donald Robert Martin Boys. In 2002, Boys invented an adjustable snake collar and tether, for the purpose of walking your pet snake. Or, slithering.

Boys found it unfortunate that most pet owners weren't able to take their pet snakes outside for fear they would escape. So, it was likely that most pet snakes rarely got enough natural sunlight, which was good for their skin and overall health. His invention aimed to remedy this situation.

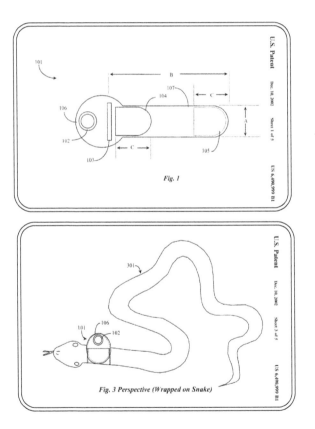

The collar itself wraps around where their "neck" sort of sits, and is fastened with Velcro. The main selling point is its adjustability.

Snakes obviously don't have any appendages, which would keep a normal collar in place. Also, their shape is always changing, what with food, growth, and their being snakes and all. Boys' invention allowed the snake to move about freely, while remaining tethered.

The tether or leash is actually is more of a rod, to keep distance, and allow the owner more steering control. Boyd refers to it as a "snake stick." At the end, it has a hook to attach to the collar. You can attach it before or after fastening the collar on your serpent. Then, you slither!

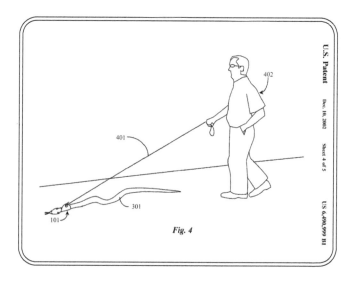

Fig. 4

The Car Flood Bag

When hurricanes hit, and sometimes, even just with heavy rains, city streets can easily turn into lazy rivers. If you haven't experienced this firsthand, you've likely seen it on the news. High waters flowing between buildings, people going around in boats as the tops of their cars float by.

Our cars are, unfortunately, one of many things in these situations that become total losses. Even if the water doesn't do the trick, the mud that gets inside the engine can easily ruin your car for good.

Daniel S. Battle, from New Orleans, invented a way to save your car. In 1980, he patented his "flood protection container for vehicles"— basically, a big plastic bag to put your car inside. Simple, yet effective!

The bag opens, with clear lines that direct you where to drive your car into it, sort of like the lines on a parking space. Then, you exit your car, and pull the sides of the bag over it, closing it off with its drawstrings. These drawstrings allow a small amount of air to escape, which prevents the bag from filling with air—and floating happily away into the sunset.

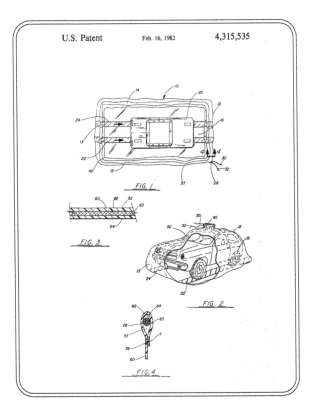

U.S. Patent   Feb. 16, 1982   4,315,535

FIG. 1

FIG. 3

FIG. 2

FIG. 4

The Early Car Visor

Automobiles weren't quite a thing yet, when an early version of (what would eventually be) the car visor was invented. This early visor was originally invented for a horse-drawn carriage. Patented by L. V. Luce in 1889, this device could be covered in cloth or leather, and was secured by a clamp to the canopy of the "vehicle." In the below illustration, you can see a woman driving a horse and buggy, with the help of the "sunshade" to keep the light out of her eyes. Just as with modern visors, it could also be easily folded up, and hidden out of sight when it wasn't needed. If only it had a mirror for a gal to check her face, that woman would, for sure, be smiling.

SUNSHADE FOR VEHICLES.

The Kissing Shield

This invention is one of the weirdest I've come across so far: the kissing shield. Basically a condom, but for kissing. I'll let your imagination run wild for a second.

The kiss shield was invented in 1998 for people who love to kiss (lots of random people, I guess), but want to avoid germs and potential diseases. It was also especially invented for "politician[s] who kisses babies." Do they still do that?

Try not to get the creeps reading the description. It's shaped sort of like a church fan, with a long handle, but the fan portion is in the shape of heart—and it's made of "a thin, flexible membrane." You use it by placing the bottom tip of the heart over your chin, the upper humps of the heart end up covering your cheeks. Once puckered up, "the user then positions the kissing shield between his lips and the lips or cheek of the individual he plans to kiss and kisses the intended recipient of his affection." And the recipient of your affection will then try to not be offended by your kissing condom.

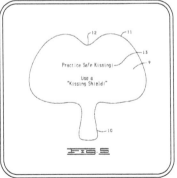

We Did That?

PAIN AND DEATH IS BEAUTY

"Today there is no excuse for a woman to grow old, unless she is ill.... If you want to keep up with this modern, wonderful world, you must be young in thought, feeling and appearance... and all you have to do is stretch out your hand to receive the magic bounty of glamour that modern science has prepared for you."

—Lily Daché, *Glamour Book*, 1956

Fashionably Dangerous History

Before you males out there shy away from this chapter—you're not getting out of it so easily. Men have had plenty of weird fashion trends of their own throughout the ages. From shoes with tips several feet long, to the proper mustache physique...weirdness, and ingenuity know no gender boundaries.

In this chapter's epigraph, Lily Daché has a very bold, and (if you'll permit me) slightly insane opinion on staying forever young and beautiful. But, while to our modern understanding this seems a ludicrous statement, I will also be bold and say that this opinion is still alive and well.

The difference is...it's simply left unsaid. It doesn't *need* to be said. What with thousands of products out there, promising youth and perfection, surgery and makeup to change a person's appearance completely, and strategically staged social media posts that influence beauty ideals and trends, well...Lily's philosophy is still embraced by our world.

While there is a glorious new wave of critics fighting ageism, body shaming, and defying beauty ideals, there is also a booming industry and culture, overflowing with toxic pressure to keep up appearances. And, new inventions and trends are constantly coming out, many, I hope we will quickly forget exist.

In this chapter, however, we can ignore current pressure and fashions, and instead, explore some of the oddest ones from the past. This way, we can see what our ancestors went through, and hopefully, gain some perspective. Though these trends are thankfully behind us, it will be interesting to explore what you, reader, think of what you see.

Do you smile and shake your head at our poor, hopeless predecessors? Do you laugh at the *riddikulus*-ness? Hopefully, many years from now, people of the future might call us out on *our* odd beauty trends!

Lipcersize

Angelina Jolie. Scarlett Johansen. Lana Del Rey. All these modern beauties have full, pouty lips that our species has prized for ages. This look has always been popular, but in the early and mid-1800s, having the "bee-stung" look on your lips was all the rage if you were a woman. As a result, many methods to achieve this look popped up.

The most accessible method was to practice lip calisthenics, repeating words beginning with the letter p throughout the day to strengthen your pucker. The most popular lipcersize chant was "peas, prunes, and prisms" with the occasional "potatoes," "paper," or "papa" added to the mix. Many young women were known to enter a room with the word "prism" fresh off their lips.

In her fabulous book on the evolution of beauty, *American Beauty*, author Lois Banner reveals that photographers of the time would even chide their subjects not to "say cheese" for their photographs, but instead recite their p-words. It's also interesting to note that Elizabeth Cady Stanton once said that "she did not bother to give feminist literature to any woman who had the 'prunes and prisms' expression on her face." Not that wanting pouty lips makes anyone anti-feminist, but we can guess she knew what she wanted her audience's priorities to be.

Healthy, rosy-colored lips have always been attractive to our species. Through the generations, you'll see there have been many crafty methods (weird to modern eyes or, um, lips) we've tried to achieve this look. From plants, to plaster, to animal fat, or worse. We may not ever fully understand *why* we want what we do, but there's no denying that beauty standards have a tendency of becoming imprinted in our psyches.

In the 1900s, a woman named Marie Montaigne penned the book, *How to be Beautiful*, and in her chapter "Beautifying the Mouth," she discusses the mouth as the key feature that expresses a woman's character. She writes, "…beautiful lips are mobile and flexible. No matter the contour, lips that are fixed and tight are never attractive." She then describes various methods of achieving the perfect lips, from keeping the corners of the mouth always turned up when feeling negative emotions, to pinching cheeks, and laughing. But not, she continues, "the constant laughter that pinches the lips and lines the cheeks." God forbid!

Nowadays, we've forgone all this hard work, and have found different strategies to enhance our pouts, like lip fillers, plumping lip gloss, and plastic surgery. But, if you're considering some of these more permanent options…now you know! Lipcersize is a cheaper, and less risky, alternative.

Among those less risky options, in 1924, a woman named Hazel Montealegre invented a device that claimed it could help women with small upper lips avoid cosmetic surgery. In order to achieve the

"Cupid's bow" shape that was popular in Hollywood at the time, her device would help "re-shape the upper lip of a person." The device worked by clamping the upper lip to an ideal lip-shaped groove, and maintained it in a flare, while the underside of the lip was also clamped outward to puff the lip even further. I think I'll take prisms and prunes.

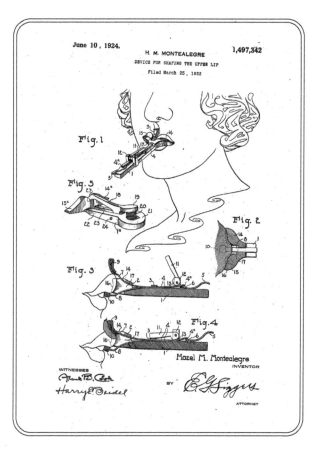

Beauty to Dye For

A geisha walks into a bar. A female employee from Crest Toothpaste is sitting there, nursing a pint after a long day. When the geisha sits down a couple stools away, they look up at each other. They smile. They stare in shock.

The geisha has pitch-black teeth, darker than a moonless midnight.

The Crest employee has teeth so white the clouds are offended.

Their smiles falter. They each look confused.

The geisha takes pity upon the Crest employee, who looks like she's going through something, and needs help warding off evil spirits. The geisha reaches into her pocket.

The Crest employee takes pity on the geisha, who looks like she's never heard of toothpaste. Crest lady reaches into her pocket.

The geisha pulls out a jar of black tooth dye. The Crest employee pulls out a packet of Crest Whitestrips.

A young geisha with blackened teeth, darker than a moonless midnight.

I obviously don't know how to tell a "person walks into a bar" joke. The fictional geisha in question has applied the ancient custom of teeth blackening, or lacquering, called *ohaguro*. Not something one sees often nowadays.

This custom is commonly linked to Japan, but has practiced in many other parts of the world, like Vietnam, China, and the Pacific Islands, as well as South America. There is no specific point in time when this custom began, but in Japan, the practice is prehistoric, and in other regions, it has been noted to exist as early as the Quin and Han dynasties (206 BCE–CE 220).

The demographics of who practiced teeth lacquering differ according to era and region, but it was mainly practiced by women, and the wealthy. It became associated with "coming of age" rituals for women, since they began applying the lacquer around the age they became eligible for marriage, and needed to attract possible suitors. These cultures believed that lacquered teeth were a true sign of beauty in a woman. And, as a young woman, who wouldn't want to be called beautiful?

A young Tonkin woman from Vietnam with blackened teeth,
by Pierre Dieulefils.

Getting Dye and Dirty

As Lisa Eldridge notes in her historical makeup book, *Face Paint*,
there are a few "whys" for this tradition. In Vietnam, it was thought
to ward off evil spirits "stemming from the belief that long, white
teeth belonged to underworld creatures, savages, and wild animals,
and that painting the teeth black would protect the wearer from
the evil spirits within them." Also, it was done for a few more
practical reasons.

In the height of this custom's popularity, I'm sad to say there was
no modern dentistry, nor were there Crest Whitestrips available
to un-yellow your teeth. So, when geishas painted their skin white,

the contrast between their white skin and yellowing teeth was unattractive. So, they joined the dark side.

The dye used to achieve this look was a concoction called *kanemizu*, which, oddly enough, helped prevent tooth decay. It was made by dissolving iron filling in vinegar with other additives, such as gallnut power, sulfuric acid, and often a combination of ink, turpentine, and wax. Not the most delicious potion for daily tasting. Some sources claim the blackened teeth came from chewing betel nut, but this is not exactly accurate, since this nut usually causes a rust-colored stain, not a black one.

A woodblock print featuring a young woman blackening her teeth (and in shock at the results, I would say).

This practice wasn't as simple as slapping on a Whitestrip, and waiting five minutes. It definitely required some maintenance. The frequency of applying the dye would vary from once a day to every few days, because it eventually faded in the mouth—though not entirely, I'll wager—there have been reports that excavated remains from the Edo period still had midnight-y teeth.

From a Western perspective, where we spend countless dollars trying to get our teeth *white*, this practice might seem confusing and odd. But, keep in mind this was, and is, an important part of many cultures—and I think I can safely say, many Western customs haven't exactly been logical either.

If you journey to Vietnam, you'll see this is still practiced in certain areas. However, in most regions, the popularity of this custom *dyed* out at the end of the nineteenth century; it was officially banned in Japan in 1870. If you want to see this custom firsthand, but can't make it to Vietnam, I recommend you keep your eyes peeled. Because you may still occasionally see black teeth…on geishas, who walk into bars.

Wooden Bathing Suits

I think women can all give a silent prayer of thanks to the swimsuit gods that this trend didn't last for long. In 1929, wooden bathing suits became all the rage, because it was believed to make swimming easier, due to the buoyancy of the wood. They were produced by Gray Harbor Lumber in Hoquiam, Washington, in the hopes that even the most hesitant swimmer would feel confident enough to jump right into the water. Gray Harbor was already renowned for profits it made in the lumber industry, and swimsuits, for some reason, became the next "logical" step in their product line.

The suits were made of spruce, thus, the ladies in the photographs earned their nickname "The Spruce Girls" (*so* close to The Spice

Girls, I know). The design was fashioned into an hourglass, cinched at the waist, with flexible planks bound together.

The Spruce Girls promoting their fashionable digs.

Don't they look like the perfect girl group? Like they're about to break out in the song "Wannabe?" The photos shown here were taken on Gray's big promotion day, when the ladies posed for photos, did video interviews about the products, and basked in the sun and sea. One video shows a designer, fitting different members of the group into different styles of the bathing suit, showcasing their versatility.

In an article by *Vintage News*, the suits were described as: "simple, cheap, and easy to make, yet fashionable and modern. In a way, they were promoting the DIY (do it yourself) and recycling for creating things. In one of the promotional videos, a girl [explains] how her father completed building a house and he had some leftover veneer. She used that veneer to make her own bathing suit." Pretty creative!

Three of The Spruce Girls (I will never tire of saying it) standing and holding an umbrella and a piece of foot-shaped wood.

There you have it: one of the roots of DIY and crafting! We might never know if these bathing suits were truly effective, providing the promised flotation, but I don't think we're missing out too badly. The first words that popped into my head when I saw the photos? *Splinters in places where splinters shouldn't be.*

Urine, Dung, Poison, Oh My!

Clear, soft skin has been a standard of beauty, probably since Eve discovered the first mirror by looking into a puddle of water. A nice complexion has never gone out of fashion, and I'd argue, it's less of a fashion and more of a permanent beauty standard.

All the way back to ancient times, having skin imperfections like acne, sallow coloring, or scars were the worst possible luck. Well, this is still an issue if you are in high school today. In her formative book, *The Royal Art of Poison,* Eleanor Herman writes that "…complexion was not simply a question of beauty. Blemishes of any kind were seen as proof of God's displeasure at sin, or worse, inner derangement." Fear of heavenly ire is a driving force behind many of our beliefs (just wait until you get to the next chapter). Such horror over these imperfections drove cosmetic inventors, and the general female public, to cringeworthy measures. In a nutshell: poison and other… unsanitary ingredients.

At the age of twenty-nine, Queen Elizabeth I was stricken with smallpox, which left small, pit-like scars all over her skin. To cover this up, she used a foundation from Italy called Venetian ceruse, also known as the spirits of Saturn. It contained a combination of egg whites, vinegar, lead, and sometimes arsenic.

In the short term, this paste could fill in the hollows, and give her skin a silvery-white appearance. But, over the long term, it led to hair loss, muscle paralysis, and a host of other issues, which probably shaved a few years off her life. In addition, the toxins left her skin even more corroded than before, so she had to cover up *even more* fiercely—a negative cycle that eventually couldn't be stopped when it became addictive to the body.

Pale is the New Pink

Lead and arsenic are two of the most popular ingredients used in makeup throughout history. To date, the amount of lead allowed in our cosmetics is still not regulated by the US government. *Gasp.* Arsenic, thankfully, is almost nonexistent in commercial products worldwide. But in its heyday, there were several arsenic-heavy stuffs on the market, promising to cure everything from freckles and pimples, to headaches, rheumatism, and low spirits!

In the early 1890s, for only a dollar, you could purchase a box of Dr. James P. Campbell's Arsenic Complexion Wafers, which contained one hundred and twenty wafers. Not too long after, in 1911, newspapers reported a young girl, named Hildegarde Walton, of St Louis, who was so eager to get rid of her acne, that she consumed several boxes of it. Spoiler alert…she died shortly after.

We might shake our heads at our ancestors' carefree use of arsenic but, back then, many didn't think it was all that bad. And, those who did still thought the risk was worth it. To their credit, there *were* results. However, like Queen Elizabeth's case, these were short term results.

Many used it, not just to get rid of acne, but to get a pale, porcelain complexion. Well, they got it! The arsenic would severely decrease their production of red blood cells, giving an extremely pale complexion…because they had developed anemia.

This controversial painting, *Madame X* by John Singer Sargent, sensualizes a woman with corpse-like skin.

An ad shown in *Cosmopolitan* magazine in 1896, lays it on really thick by promising to "give the complexion and indescribable brilliancy and lend to every young lady a charm of person which makes her adorable." So, it could even change your personality, apparently. Not wrong—but it wouldn't be in an adorable way. Prolonged usage caused severe mood swings.

L = O = V = E = L = Y !

She was certainly an exquisitely lovely creature. Nothing could have been added to enhance her beauty. She compelled admiration, and was an object of worship. This is the **universal result** of the use of

DR. CAMPBELL'S
SAFE ARSENIC COMPLEXION WAFERS

and **Fould's Medicated Arsenic Complexion Soap.** These two **World Famous Beautifiers** transform the most sallow skin into **radiant** health; remove **pimples**; clear the face of **freckles** and tan; give the complexion **an indescribable brilliancy,** and lend to every young lady **a charm of person** which makes her **ADORABLE.** Wafers by mail 50c. and $1.00 per Box. 6 large boxes $5.00. Soap by mail 50c. per cake.

Address H. B. Fould, 214 6th Ave., New York.
SOLD BY DRUGGISTS EVERYWHERE.

It's interesting to note that in the advertisement they talk about their model in the past tense...

On the label of Dr. James P. Campbell's Arsenic Complexion Wafers package, there was a guarantee spelled out in all caps: GUARANTEED ABSOLUTELY SAFE. You can trust a doctor, after all, can't you?

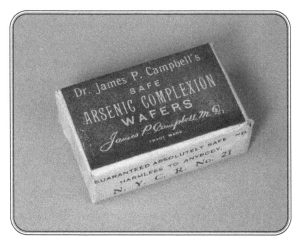

The original product in all its poisonous glory.

The Face of Beauty

Arsenic had many shady friends. Other exciting ingredients you could find in skin remedies included human or animal urine, dung, fat, organs, blood—shall I keep going?

In *The Royal Art of Poison* Herman reveals: "Some women filled in smallpox pits with a mixture of turpentine, beeswax, and human fat. Where to find human fat? You could buy it at your local apothecary or, cutting out the middleman, directly from the town executioner, who sliced it from the still-warm corpses of condemned criminals." People and animals fresh off Death's to-do list were very valuable commodities. Ladies in Queen Elizabeth's time, who wanted soft skin, were urged to push their hands through the open wounds of animals killed while on hunting excursions, and rub it all over the areas they wanted softer skin or to cure warts.

A crafty sixteenth-century physician and alchemist, Maister Alexis of Piedmont, believed devotedly in dung. His prescription to cure pimples goes thus: "In the month of Maie, when oxen goe to grasse, or bee at pasture, ye shall take of their dung, not too freshe, nor too drie, then distill it faire and softlie into some vessel or glasse, of the which will come a water, without savour or evil stench, which will be verie excellent good, to take off all manner of spots or blemishes in the face, if you wash with it morning and evening." Remember: semi-fresh dung only.

The good Maister also recommended a concoction of powdered mice dung, with a spoonful of sugar to choke it down, "for him that spitteth blood by having some vaine of his breast broken," to be taken before breakfast and before bedtime. My two favorite times to eat mice droppings.

Urine was also another early "cleanser." The sixteenth-century English surgeon Willian Bullein prescribed a mixture of "distilled water of honey, strong vinegar, milk, and the urine of a boy." I wonder how that conversation would go—imagine asking your little brother why he had to pee in a jar.

Our trusted doc, Maister Alexis, again recommended to "take earth and knead it with dog's pisse, and laie upon the warts and they will drie up and consume awaie." Ladies and gentlemen, I present to you: the early face mask. As Herman notes, this waste product is still used in modern products. Let's look at a few of the ingredients that have stood the test of time and sanitation.

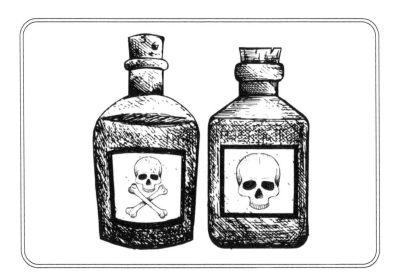

MODERN COSMETICS

Questionable ingredients are not just in products from ages past, but can still be found in makeup currently on the market. And not just drugstore brands, but the fancy, expensive ones too. Don't think rust could possibly be in your forty-dollar lipstick? Sorry to be the bearer of bad news. Let's look at lipstick, the one makeup product we unintentionally end up ingesting. The following list are ingredients still used in today's makeup, and how they are abbreviated on the label so you can find them yourself.

Bugs

The insect "cochineal" has been used to color a variety of products since Cleopatra's time. It's used to give the red color in lipstick. The pigment comes from the crushed bodies of pregnant females. Fun fact: it takes about ninety thousand bugs to create just one kilogram of cochineal powder. Cochineal also appears in items like yogurt, fruit juice, nail polish, and blush. Labels to look for: carmine, carminic acid, and cochineal extract. Thousands of another insect, the "lac" bug, are killed for use in nail and hair products. Labels to look for: shellac.

Rust

How does red pigment get into lipstick? If not the above insects, we use rust, or sometimes both, in blush, lipstick, and other cosmetics. Labels to look for: iron oxide or any five-digit number starting with "774," such as 77491.

Lead and Other Metals

Lead and co. are found in commodities like lipwear, toothpaste, eyeliner, sunscreen, eyedrops, and more. I found it interesting that it was so difficult for me to find out how we, consumers, can actually identify lead, and other harmful metals. There aren't many resources, unless you dig, which *leads* me to the conclusion the cosmetic industry *doesn't* want them to be easily identified. Sorry to spoil the grand scheme. Labels to look for: lead acetate, chromium (transition metal), thimerosal (mercury compound), calomel or mercurio (fancy names for mercury).

Animals and Their Parts

All that glitters is…fishy. Powdered fish scales are being used in products like eyeshadow, nail polish, and bath products to create a pearly, crystalline shimmer. Labels to look for: guanine and hypoxanthine. A man named Umesh Soni, a Mumbai-based microbiologist, founded the cosmetic company named Cowpathy whose sole mission is to create products using cow dung and "cowe pisse," as Maister Alexis might refer to it, since it is believed to have healing properties. Labels to look for: anything Cowpathy.

Unclog Your Bust

Trying to title this section had my brain all…stopped up. I almost called it "The Boob Booster." Had to get that off my chest. But I digress before I've even begun. Let's start over.

Oh, men. Inventors of high heels, bras, and all that is uncomfortable for women. The very first patent with the clearly stated purpose of breast enhancement appeared in 1889. The patent application was submitted by a man named Harry L Miller, hailing from Chicago, Illinois. The purpose of the Bust Developer, he wrote, was "to fill out shrunken and underdeveloped tissues, form a rounded, plump, perfectly developed bust, producing a beautiful figure."

The contraption itself is a "bell-shaped dome," which in all honesty resembles a fancy toilet plunger. Just like them, it also has a straight handle extending up, and is used in the exact same manner. Except, the only thing you're unclogging from your body is more boobage.

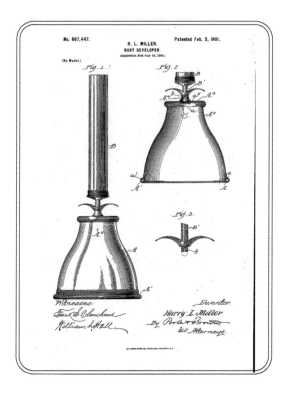

The users are instructed to place the dome around "the part to be treated" tightly, so no air escapes. Once they place their finger or thumb over the device's opening, blocking all air, they pull on it, causing suction. In the end, "the result [is] that the supply of blood to the parts being treated is increased. The repetition of this treatment tends to an increased growth or an enlargement of the bust." An ornamental way of saying, "Yeah, so whatever you do to the toilet, just do that on your chest!"

When advertised to the public in the Sears, Roebuck & Co. catalog, it was given a more appealing name, The Princess Bust Developer, and was sold as a package deal with two other products. One was jar of Bust Cream or Food (the actual product name, I guess they're indecisive like me), and a liquid concoction called Genuine Fleur De

Lis Bust Expander was thrown in for free. The price? You could get all three for the unbeatable price of $1.46. In today's money that's about forty-one dollars.

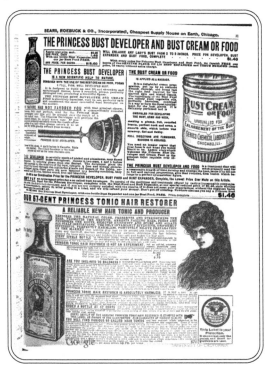

Another breast enhancement invention was called Lady Bountiful's Vacuum Pump. It had a different design, but was used for the same purpose as the plunger. A key difference? It was powered by water. Instead of a long handle, it had a flexible plastic tube a few feet long, and a cone shape that fit over the breast. The directions specified to use it in your bathroom, and in a few simple steps:

1. Attach vacuum unit [i.e. the long plastic tube] to the cold-water faucet.

2. Turn the water on—full force.

3. Place plastic cup snugly over breast.

4. Place thumb over the small opening near the cup, and hold the thumb there, until the vacuum (created by the flow of water) pulls the breast out fully into the cup.

5. After the breast has been pulled into the cup, release thumb suddenly, and allow breast to return to original position.

I would love to see how flooded the bathroom floor was after the first use.

The breast enhancement craze is a beauty standard that has not died out through the years. The methods have merely gotten craftier and more high tech, with surgical alteration being the permanent solution most popular now.

Before we end this section, I wanted to mention an exquisitely cringeworthy book written in the 1970s titled *Natural Bust Enlargement with Total Mind Power: How to Use the Other 90% of Your Mind to Increase the Size of Your Breasts*. This book attempts to teach its readers how they can *think* their breasts bigger. With their mindpower alone. Thankfully, I was not able to find this book being sold anywhere on the market. Small blessings. But, if you happen to have a copy and this mindpower method works for you…let me know, won't you?

Mouche Ado about Fashion

LE MATIN
La Dame a sa Toilete.

An etching of a young beauty-marked woman by
French artist Gilles Edme Petit.

Rarely do both men and women take up the same fashion trends, but
the case of *mouches* is special.

It once was a popular practice for both men and women alike to
decorate their faces with a black patch or, when on a woman, "beauty
mark." These were called *mouches*. In French, this word means "fly"—
which makes sense, given the beauty marks were black and usually
about the same size as one. Also common, however, was that the
patches were also cut in a variety of shapes, from hearts, to crescent
moons, and more.

This fashion can be traced back to the time of the Roman poet Ovid, but grew in popularity in the sixteenth and seventeenth centuries, in France and the UK, and again, later, during America's early Hollywood era. It was mainly practiced by the upper class who could afford to accessorize. The mouches could be made from silk, velvet, satin, or taffeta—not cheap materials to acquire during its heyday. An option for people of limited income was made of mouse skin. There is even a street in Venice called Calle de Moschete, where these accessories were once sold.

Sources suggest many reasons this became so popular for both sexes. Yes, the patches were a fashion statement, but they were also used for more practical purposes to cover up smallpox scars, blemishes, or when you were simply having a bad face day. The contrast and *pow* of the dark mark was believed to make you appear more attractive.

Samuel Pepys, a diarist in the mid-seventeenth century, who is known for the accurate descriptions of everyday life in his notebooks, once wrote about when his own wife began imitating this trend. "My wife seemed very pretty today," he writes, "it being the first time I had given her leave to wear a black patch." Not long after, when he was recovering from bout of illness, it looks like he invaded her boudoir. He wrote that he was, "Up pretty well again, but my mouth very scabby, my cold being going away, so that I was forced to wear a great black patch." You see, even Mr. Pepy's wanted to look purty.

As the popularity of patching grew, it also became a way to show social status—married women might wear the patch on their right cheek, available women on their left, and mistresses next to their mouths. Oftentimes, the placement of the mouche acted as a code for secret lovers. Entire books were written on this art, containing all the codes and meanings behind the placement.

The Patch Party

In another vein, patching became a method to display which political party you supported. This could be the party a woman's husband supported, but often it was the lady's preference. There you go…an important piece of fashion for women during a time when they did not get a say, nor the chance to voice their opinions. We women will always find a way.

The English essayist and playwright Joseph Addison wrote about this in the satirical newspaper he co-founded, *The Spectator*. His piece covers these "party patches," as he calls them. One evening, when he attended the opera, he noticed groups of women sharing "hostile glances" with one another, and noticed that their faces were patched differently. Some had placed their mark on the left side of their forehead, others on the right.

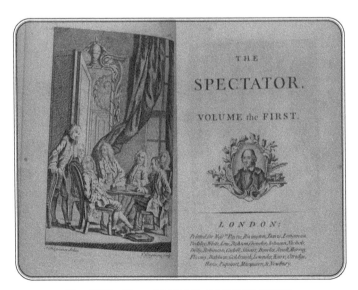

The 1788 edition of Addison's satirical newspaper.

"Upon inquiry," he writes, "I found, that the body of Amazons on my right hand were Whigs, and those on my left, Tories. And that those who had placed themselves in the middle boxes were a neutral party, whose faces had not yet declared themselves." Addison further adds a twist of humor in his article by describing a woman who had a natural birth mole on her forehead that caused much confusion among the ladies. "Rosalina, a famous Whig partisan, has most unfortunately a very beautiful mole on the Tory part of her forehead; which… has occasioned many mistakes, and given an handle to her enemies to misrepresent her face, as though it had revolted from the Whig interest." I think I would have caused a great deal of confusion as well, since I am quite be-freckled.

There were many naysayers regarding the use of patches, of course. Clergy and other members of society believed the practice was vain, and that vanity was, of course, the root of evil. It was banned, and brought back many times over the years, it's last renaissance came during the early days of the Hollywood film era. It's been quite a while since beauty patching has buzzed our way, but who knows! Just like flies, fashion trends always have a way of coming back.

Malepolish

Trends have a boomerang-y nature. They usually always come back. At this writing, men wearing nail polish has become in vogue once more, but many think it is a new development. However, men have been wearing nail polish, or malepolish as I call it, since about 3,200 BCE.

In Babylonia, Rome, and China, warriors were known to paint their nails, lips, and hair black in preparation for battle. In China, they've been painting their nails for over five thousand years. But, it might be more accurate to say they "dyed" them since the concoction was more liquid than modern polishes we're used to. It was usually made from a combo of egg whites, gelatin, and beeswax. More commonly, though, they use "kohl" which could be made from lead or charcoal.

Nail tinting was done mainly by the upper class and, depending on the color, to show social status. In other words: the darker your nails, the cooler you were. Kind of like today. Dark nails make you look badass. I think I know what color I'm choosing for my next *man*icure.

Headdress Over Heels

In the early 1400s, the width of one's headwear was all the rage. The more shade you could get over your toes, the better. But later in the century, this transitioned to vertical, skyward growth in an alarming fashion trend. One fashionable example was the hennin.

The hennin was a headdress in the shape of a cone or unicorn horn, usually with a thin veil draping from the top. As the fashion grew in popularity, the height of the hennin would reach nearly four feet tall. Women had to use sturdy pins, ribbons, or even glue, some sources say, to keep it strapped onto their heads.

The headdress was worn at a slight tilt, about a forty-five-degree angle, covering all of a woman's hair. And since the hennin rested so far back on the head, women would often pluck their hairline back, so that not a single strand showed. Having a very large forehead was trendy, so many would also pluck off their eyebrows too!

Hennin popularity started in Europe, and spread quickly to the English courts. As with most high fashion, these steeple headdresses were reserved solely for upper-class women. How could you weave or tend a field whilst wearing a precariously placed four-foot headdress?

As different styles of the hennin developed, you could find variations such as one that looked like a Turkish fez, or another called the butterfly hennin, where two cones or wires were used as the peaks, making you look like you had big bunny ears under your veil. Or like you had the Queen of Hearts' oversized, heart-shaped head. It was simply high fashion.

Mine Is Bigger than Yours

As the headwear of the ladies grew taller, men were waging their own battle of "whose is bigger." And no, I'm not referring to *that*. Dirty mind. Well, maybe I kind of am.

In the Middle Ages, around the 1360s, the male fashion trend for long, pointy shoes grew in England. In fact, it became popular just after the Black Death killed a large chunk of the population, so it's probable that men wanted something a little lighthearted and frilly to brighten up their lives. Retail therapy, if you will. These pointy shoes became popularly known as *poulaines*, translating from French roughly to "shoes worn in the Polish fashion," because that's where they originated.

As the years went by (it stuck around for about three hundred years!), the tips of the shoes grew longer, and longer, making it almost impossible for men to walk. Some tips recorded reached as long as two feet! Starting from the tip of their real toes. If the average male foot is about nine inches, they were ambling around with nearly three feet. That's a lot to carry around! You were basically walking around in leather skis.

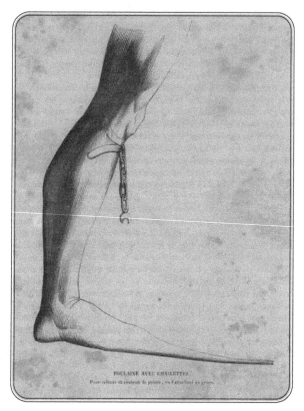

POULAINE AVEC CHAUSETTES

Some extensions grew so heavy that they had to be
supported by chains strapped to the knees.

The poulaines were—like so much of fashion—a status symbol. The
longer your tips were, the wealthier you were. Men could barely walk
around in these shoes, which showed they were fancy enough that
they didn't need to do any physical labor.

As with most daring fashion, the church and government grew
shocked at the sexual significance of these shoes, and laws we're put in
place to regulate them. You see, many men would stuff their shoe tips
with wool, whalebones, or other materials in order to keep them—*ach
em*—erect. Some would even paint their shoe extensions a fleshy, skin-
toned color. Yes, the Middle Agers were sexier than we thought.

This gravity-defying footwear made a soft reappearance in the 1950s with the winklepicker shoes—though this style is much more subdued. But it made a large and in charge comeback recently, in the early 2000s, in Matehuala, Mexico. Men added flare to their cowboy boots in the same traditional fashion. But some of these shoe styles—if one can truly call them shoes—reach several feet long. The extensions usually curve upward in the same way you might imagine elf shoes to look. Some high fashion designers even started featuring them on their runways. But, as with any trend, it's only a matter of time before it fades. After all…what goes up must come down. *Wink.*

Four-Legged Panty Hose

It looks like a pair of tights made specially for the aliens Kang and Kodos Johnson from *The Simpsons*, but inventor Annette Pappas had a different species in mind. The Panty Hose x3 is a four-legged panty hose product meant to provide ladies with an extra leg wherever they go.

You would wear them normally (one leg in each hole), and tuck in the extra two. That way, in the case of a rip or little snag, you could just nip away to the bathroom and rotate another leg on. Simple! Now, if only I could get Kang and Kodos out of my head.

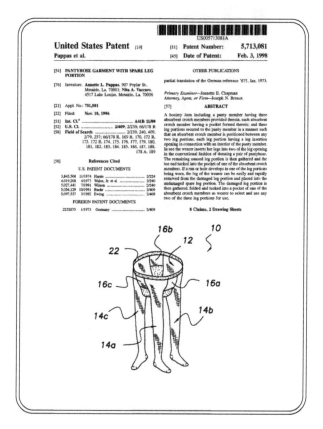

Suck It in, Dude

It will make all women quite gleeful to know that there was a moment—a very quick, white hot moment—in history where men got a little taste of what we women had to go through for fashion. In the late 1700s and early 1800s, having a thin waist was very in vogue, not just for women, but for men as well! The high fashion of the time for men included very form-fitting trousers and jackets. But, what about those who needed a little help sucking it in? A little figure shaping? Well, around 1820, men began wearing corsets for the very first time in history. I'll let that sink in for a moment, guys.

Reast's Invicorator Belt being modeled.

One particular corset brand for men, Reast's Patent Invicorator Belt, expounded on the many *manly* benefits it would bring: "Besides showing off the figure and enabling the tailor to ensure an effective fit and distinguished appearance, this combined Belt Corset is a necessity to most men for the promotion of health and comfort, together with an upright, soldierly bearing."

Corsets are notorious for the damage they can cause to one's internal organs, but that's apparently not the case here. "It expands the chest. It supports the spine, and holds the figure erect. It protects the lungs and kidneys from cold. It support the stomach." The advertisement then goes on to demonstrate a (probably fictional) conversation between two doctors trying on the corset. (Excuse me, *belt*.)

> Dr. Wilson says—"The Belt made for me by Reast's Patentee is the most comfortable I have worn. It gives great support to the muscles of the back, and will be found very useful to prevent stooping."

> Dr. Haddon says—"I am now wearing your Belt Corset, and must say that it gives wonderful support. I shall certainly not fail to recommend it to my patients."

> Recommended by doctors for gentlemen. Reast's Patent Invicorator Belt.

As I'm sure you have guessed, this trend did not last very long. It eventually became associated with Dandyism—being a man overly concerned with refinement and fashion. This characteristic was seen as too feminine, so men's corsets uncinched their clasp on fashion very shortly thereafter.

We Did That?

ODD JOBS

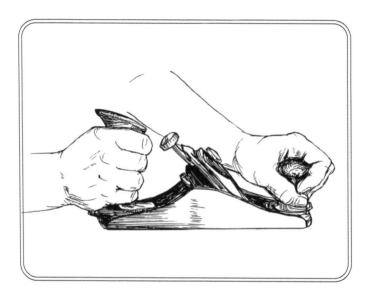

"Whatever your life's work is, do it well."

—Martin Luther King Jr.

Because Someone Has to Do It

Somebody has to do those odd jobs. You know—the ones that are too niche to learn through a traditional college education. The career track you sort of just fall into with a twist of fate. Shark tank cleaner? Elephant costume stylist? There's a human for the job.

Some trades spring up out of popular demand, and fade away in a few years, and some are necessary for survival (until we find a machine to do the job). But, one thing is constant: odd jobs tell us a lot about the ingenuity and skill of the human race. People are talented! Many cunning.

Also, these professions say a lot about their specific time period: the influence of religion, the fads of the people, and the state of the working world. So much can be learned from looking into the past. Though technology, science, and simple modernity have erased many of these jobs from our classifieds and help wanted listings, here—if only for a chapter—we'll live vicariously through those odd balls who decided to be that "someone" who has to do it.

Knocker Upper

Through cobbled streets, cold and damp, the knocker-upper man is creeping. Tap, tapping on each windowpane, to keep the world from sleeping...

—Mike Canavan

Requirements: Pole, frozen peas, immunity to crankiness

Job Status: Extinct

I know this odd job sounds like someone who professionally impregnates women, but alas, it is not. A knocker upper was an early version of an alarm clock, in human form, that arose in the mid to late 1800s. People who had to rise early for work would pay knocker uppers to come around and tap on their windows to wake them up bright and early. Most customers had industrial jobs, which required a strict and early schedule. But not many could afford to buy a clock, which was usually too pricey for their paygrade.

What the knocker uppers would do is use long poles to reach high-up windows they would tap, or, they'd shoot peas at them through a straw. They didn't want to be waking anyone for free, so these methods were just loud enough to get the job done, but quiet enough not to wake the neighbor one window down.

But who woke up the knocker uppers? The people of the day often had the same question. Here is a common tongue-twister-like rhyme that arose:

> We had a knocker-up, and our knocker-up had a knocker-up
>
> And our knocker-up's knocker-up didn't knock our knocker up
>
> So our knocker-up didn't knock us up
>
> 'Cos he's not up.

But to answer this plaguing question, many simply adapted a vampiric schedule. They slept in the day, waking up in the early evening, ready to start their shift in a few hours.

This trade was eventually put to bed by mechanical alarm clocks. Seth E. Thomas patented the first in October 1876, but that didn't *really* stop these guys. This job was a widely popular all the way until the 1930s, occasionally, knocker-uppers could be hired as late as the 1970s. After that, it officially hit the hay as a paid profession. Though I would argue the profession still exists. When I was a wee lass, my mom was my personal knocker-upper every morning before school. Until I discovered what an electric alarm clock (and responsibility) was. Now, every morning I'm stuck listening to a ringtone that's too soothing to wake me up, but too perky to ignore and go back to sleep. I think you know which one I'm talking about. Sigh. Those good old days.

The Thirty-Year Virgin

Requirements: Female virgin, young, preferably noble-born, likes fire

Job Status: Extinct

In ancient Rome, girls between the age of six and ten—the time when my priorities were Britney Spears and saving up for a Walkman—were selected for a thirty-year term of service to the goddess, Vesta. These girls also had to have all their limbs (minor detail), and be born of noble parents. The job duties of a Vestal Virgin? To guard and tend to an ancient flame. Their mission was to serve the goddess Vesta, and tend to her shrine—keeping the flame burning—with some other miscellaneous tasks, such as ministering during Vesta's feast days in June.

The Greek-Roman essayist, Plutarch, wrote about these Virgins, saying, "Some are of the opinion that these vestals had no other business than the preservation of [the sacred] fire; but others conceive[d] that they were keepers of other divine secrets, concealed from all but themselves." *Not a bad gig*, you might think. These women were absolutely revered in their society, often given freedoms other women weren't allowed, such as owning property. But the price of this privilege was steep.

If they lost their virginity, or made any minor error, the punishment was severe. Loss of their virgin status would mean they were brutally beaten, and then buried alive. Some sources even say they were force-fed molten lava.

Other, more minor offenses, such as letting the fire go out, also came with great consequence. After all, the continuously burning fire was believed to be tied to the fortune of the entire city. Neglecting this sacred duty could bring tragedy to Rome.

This job (for a job it was) remained a central part of Roman culture, until 394 CE, when the Christian emperor Theodosius I freed the Vestas from what he believed was a pagan ritual. Both their job, with all its perks, and the sacred fire, were snuffed out. You can still see the ruins of the Atrium Vitae, where they lived and worked, in the Roman Forum today.

The Foretaster

Requirements: Mouth, stomach, low self-preservation instincts, puts safety third

Job Status: Active

The ancient profession of food taster, officially known by its Latin name praegustator, or simply foretaster, has always been a bit of a gamble. While there are many dangerous jobs out there (police officer, construction worker, retail), this is a job you sign up for *knowing* you could surely die. Perhaps you already knew from history books that royals often had their food tasted, but did you know people would sign up for it? It was not just poor slaves who were thrust into this role.

As the name suggests, foretasters would get paid to taste the dishes of royalty or the rich, so that, if the food was poisoned, the taster would die instead of their employer. Basically, taking the bullet. The food bullet. Why would anyone sign up for this? Well, we can guess these professionals thought that the benefits of this job outweighed it's one major drawback. After all, you do get to enjoy some of the finest cuisines—food literally fit for an emperor or king. Also, out of loyalty to the ruler—blah blah. It also paid well. What is death to that, eh?

One food taster remembered throughout history was a servant and eunuch named Halotus. He was the chief steward and praegustator for the Roman Emperor Claudius. The reason Halotus is remembered is quite ironic—he failed at his job. Spoiler alert.

His boss, the emperor Claudius ended up being murdered. It was believed he was poisoned, and Halotus was the primary suspect in the investigation. Shocker, that is. But strangely enough, there wasn't enough evidence to convict Halotus. So, he lived out the rest of his life in luxury. (Claudius' successor ended up giving him a prestigious position…fishy, don't you think?)

Just because this odd job is ancient, however, does not mean it has died out! *Ba dun tsss*. Rulers from Napoleon and Queen Elizabeth I, to Hitler, Turkish President Recep Tayyip Erdogan, and US President Barack Obama, are known to have had food tasters. Poison is the stealthiest weapon of all; it accomplishes its task without revealing a killer's face, and is sometimes so subtle that the cause of death is believed to be something else. As long as there are people in positions of power who are protected by strong walls, bodyguards, and the like, poison will unfortunately always be a tool—to the detriment of daring praegustators.

Speaking of jobs that require tasting questionable things, here is one more.

Dog Food Taster: It's logical to assume that whichever species food is intended for should be the one to taste it, but when did life ever make sense? Human dog food tasters exist to evaluate the flavor, texture, and smell of dog food, in comparison to other brands. It's interesting, yet, disturbing to note that we humans are more likely to buy food and treats that smell good to *us*, not necessarily our dogs. So, most of the artificial scents, dyes, and flavors that are included in dog foods are actually for our benefit. Did I mention there are people out there who have to eat *dog food* to earn a living?

The Night Soil Men

Requirements: Doesn't mind getting down and dirty, dedication to getting shit done

Job Status: Active

Before there was plumbing, there were only a few options for getting rid of our, *ahem*, human waste. We could dump it into a river, or bury it in a hole. In cities, however, options were more limited. Cities were not the most enjoyable places to live pre-sewer systems. With few means of getting rid of our junk, it often found its way into the streets in the form of deep cesspools in the ground.

How was this managed? Who were we to turn to? Well, when shit literally piled up, the night soil men came to the rescue! They are also known by the name *gong farmer*, and, in ancient Rome, *stercorarius*. For those of you unfamiliar with the term, "night soil" is a polite way of referring to human waste. These independent contractors would come around in their carts, collecting our poop, and other miscellaneous rubbish. Just like getting water out of a well, they would collect the sludge, bucket by bucket. When there was excess at the bottom that couldn't be collected via bucket, the laborers would have to descend on a ladder into the depths of the hole. They were in deep shit!

An eighteenth-century ad by a "Nightman & Rubbish Carter" seeking an apprentice.

It wasn't uncommon for the night soil men to be compensated with a bottle of gin. But there were other profits to be made as well. Once their tubs and carts were full, they would haul their loads outside of the city. The trash would be sorted for anything that could be repurposed or profited from, and the night soil would be sold at a decent price to farmers for crop fertilizer. The cycle of life: we eat the food, we poop the food, our poop fertilizes the new food.

"Muckmen" or "gong-fermors" were other names used to refer to the night soil men in the past, but there is a modern Haitian word for this job as well: *bayakou*. Yes, this job is still alive today. In a *National Geographic* article by photojournalist Andrea Bruce, she provides an interesting lens into this profession. Bayakou, in her words, are "laborers who empty latrines." Sanitation is still a deadly threat, and sewage still a system in progress in Haiti, so what these laborers do is visit the waste site—usually a hole dug in the ground—and insert the waste into bags (usually by hand), and cart it off in a truck. A similar procedure as practiced by the night soil men of the past. One thing is certain—even though it was, and still is, an unpleasant job, it is a necessary one. But sometimes, the oddest jobs are the most needed.

Professional Cursers

Requirements: Literate, can get creative, interested in the dark arts

Job Status: Active, if you're into that sort of thing

If you had been robbed, cheated, or were simply pissed off at someone in ancient Rome, you had to take matters into your own hands. Or, rather, put matters into the hands of the supernatural. At the time, Rome didn't have a formal police force, aside from the night watch. So, what better way to seek justice than to involve the gods, and curse the person who wronged you? How about etching their name with a really nasty jinx into a piece metal or stone that will survive thousands of years?

This practice became such a hot commodity, that it was clear an official occupation was needed. A professional. No more of this *amateur* cursing going around. This is how the odd job of "curse-tablet maker" came about. All you had to do was pop 'round to your local curser, and they would carve the one you wanted, or even supply standard cursing language, if you weren't very poetic. To achieve maximum cursage, the malediction would often be written backwards. It cost extra to add serpents, or the likeness of Medusa.

Once your tablet was ready, you would either leave it wedged into the cursee's walls, into their floorboards, or leave it at a temple or holy site. Many tablets have been discovered over the years in sanctuaries all over the world.

I got to see some of these tablets myself, this past summer, when I visited the city of Bath, in England. In the Roman baths, which was both a gathering place and holy site dedicated to the goddess Sulis Minerva, there was an extensive collection of coins that had been cast into the water there over a thousand years ago. On these coins, or thin tablets made of lead, the cursers called upon the goddess Sulis

Minerva—the patron of many things, including justice—to bring ill health or misfortune upon the person they named. Here are some curses that have been translated:

> "I curse Tretia Maria and her life and mind and memory and liver and lungs mixed up together, and her words, thoughts and memory; thus may she be unable to speak what things are concealed, nor be able."

> "Docimedis has lost two gloves and asks that the thief responsible should lose their minds and eyes in the goddess' temple."

> "May he who carried off Vilbia from me become liquid as the water. May he who so obscenely devoured her become dumb."

For that last one, I think we can assume this person was talking about an animal that was stolen from them. Unless "he who carried off Vilbia" was a cannibal and kidnapped this person's servant or child, in which case—may he become as liquid as water!

Cursing spread to areas outside Roman territories, however. In Amathus, an ancient city in Cyprus, which is now an archeological site, a stone tablet was discovered, with this curse carved on it:

"May your penis hurt when you make love."

OoOoo. *Burn.* Pun intended.

Armmpit Plucker

Requirements: Attention to detail, ability to handle oneself in hairy situations

Job Status: Extinct

While we're on the subject of ancient Roman baths, and things that sting... Visiting the baths was similar to the experience of going to a spa. After taking a long dip in the hot mineral water, you would get pampered in the adjoining rooms (think of them sort of like fancy locker rooms, since they were separated by sex). Once you detoxed in a room of steam, and got a nice rub down from one of the slaves there, you could also get groomed. And let me tell you, Romans were almost as bad as millennials are when it comes to removing body hair.

The bath guilds employed people whose sole job was to pluck the hair from your armpits. Going hairless was extremely fashionable in the first and second century CE, so their services were widely used. They usually advertised vocally (and loudly). Their racket became so commonplace in society, that Lucius Annaeus Seneca, the tutor for young Emperor Nero, wrote "...and the hair plucker with his shrill and high-pitched voice, continually shrieking in order to be noticed. He's never quiet, except for when he's plucking armpits and forcing his customers to shriek instead of him." Now, I don't know any sadistic person who plucks armpit hair. No, we have wax and laser hair removal technicians to hear us shriek instead. Sometimes, things never change.

Knock-Knobbler

Requirements: Bouncer attitude, loves church

Job Status: Extinct

Back in the days, when going to church was a requirement of religion for many, there existed a sort of bouncer for those who got too rowdy during services. They were known as knock knobblers. Not a name you hear every day. Another title they were often known by was "dog catcher," but their job duties often expanded beyond those boundaries. How many stray dogs could there possibly be to catch, after all?

From misbehaving children to those sermon-crashing stray dogs—a knock knobbler's job was to get them out. They were employed by the church to keep order and quiet. But in their downtime, they had long sticks to poke anyone they caught snoozing. They were most active in England, during the Elizabethan era, snoozing their own way out of existence not long after.

Plumassier

Requirements: Feathers, artistic tendencies

Job Status: Active

The profession of plumassier is a special kind of bird. Plumassiers are craftspersons who design ornamental feathers. Well, I guess nature designs them. Plumassiers design the designed feathers! All for the love of avian fashion, these skilled artisans collect, treat, and design their fluffy products by hand. Not only do you have to really like feathers, but you have to have an artistic eye. Accessorizing with feathers goes back all the way to the Stone Age, and like all art forms, it has morphed. From ancient wall art to headdresses, fans, ball gowns, and feathered pumps you see on the runway today.

Despite the stereotype of women being more fashion-inclined, originally this trade was dominated by men—gendered work exists even in the artisan world. During an interview with one of the last few plumassier workshops in France named Masion Lemarié, the journalist, Merle Patchett, discovered that before 1776, "plumassiers were considered an old and male community." This status was influenced by, of course, men. "The powerful and patriarchal urban craft guilds, of which plumassiers were one," Patchett continues, "had conspired to confine apprenticeships for girls to a narrow range of trades." Usually, the work assigned to women consisted of work one could do at home. Nothing that required skill with machinery. So detail-oriented, artisanal, in-shop work was given to men. That is how not just the plumassier craft, but "the privileges, the work identity, and the customary rights, trappings of artisanal work values, [almost] became the exclusive domain of skilled men."

A plumassier workshop in France, as depicted by Diderot d'Alembert.

I believe it goes without saying that feathercraft is a very niche calling. Even at the height of its industry, there were not many in the flock. Today, even less so, with only a handful of individuals that answer the call. Maison Lemarié is one of the last businesses that specializes in this trade. It was founded in 1875, and has become so notable that they've been working with one of their chief clients, Chanel, since the 1960s.

Using Paris as an example, by the end of the nineteenth century, there were hundreds of plumassiers in the city. You could walk the streets, and count dozens of bird species on the hats, dresses, and other accessories of women. The value of feathers was just under that of diamonds. In the *Titanic*, at the bottom of the ocean there are about forty cases of feathers estimated at over 2.3 million dollars in value. Now, a hundred years later, there are barely a handful of plumassiers left—as of this writing, less than five.

How did this soaring trade lose its wings? It's not terribly difficult to guess that, just like with the fur industry, people finally came to realize beauty had a price that was too high to pay. Many of the fashion victims of this trade were becoming extinct–and others were simply being slaughtered by the hundreds for the sake of fancy hats. Then, in 1918, the Migratory Bird Treaty Act was passed, protecting all non-game birds from being hunted or sold. The fashion itself became a stigma, and lost its hype. But this ancient practice—as we know from the continued pulse of plumassier trade—is not totally lost. With artificial options and vintage feathers available, you can still find the art of feathercraft peeking its beak into the fashion world at large.

Haruspex

Requirements: In touch with spiritual side, strong stomach

Job Status: Active

If the name of this job odd job sounds scary, that's probably appropriate. A haruspex was a religious official in ancient times, who was trained to "read" the entrails of sacrificed animals, seeking divine meaning.

The haruspices' practice was also called by other names (with about the same level of appeal), like extispicy and haruspicy. The ritual was performed when someone requested input from the spiritual realm—to give them a sign and/or confirmation they were on the right path. Any government official or general about to go to war were bound to visit their local augurate. If a god had been angered, it was the haruspex's duty to determine which god was offended, and what the right offering would be to appease them. Usually, when the entrails were tossed into the fire, how exactly they burned was important to observe as well.

This unpleasant practice can be traced all the way back to the second millennium BCE, and is descended from the Etruscans. It is a branch of augury (a term some are more familiar with), a form of divination, accomplished by reading signs found in nature. Other very popular activities of augurates were to observe how birds would take flight, noting what formations or patterns they created, or the pecking patterns of a group of chickens. Augurates also found signs in lightning bolts, and the sounds of thunder.

Why was this done exactly? Well, since augury is meant to observe the signs nature gives, the theory behind killing the animal was that, once it was sacrificed to a god, it would become part of the god (making it divine). Once the animal's insides were revealed, it was like the haruspex was getting a sneak peek into their god's mind.

Despite the needless death of the animals and cringe-worthiness of the job, haruspicy is still practiced in some very remote areas of the world. You know, you have likely practiced a vague form of augury yourself. Have you ever broken a wish bone with someone to see who was luckier? Cracked a walnut shell on New Year's Eve? You're guilty of being an augurate!

Knife Grinder

Requirements: Knave for sharp blades, portable grindstone

Job Status: Active

The job of knife grinder, or sharpener man, has been known to exist at least as early as the 1600s, though probably dates back earlier. What is a knife grinder, you ask? It is someone who goes around with a portable grindstone to offer their sharpening service to the people of their town. They will sharpen knives, scissors, and any other utensil that needs a keen edge. They usually have a bell tied to their cart, so that the townsfolk know when they are passing by. Many people will rush out to get their dulled tools sharpened, and many knife grinders have frequent customers like restaurants, hotels, and families.

This profession might seem too old-fashioned to still be around, but there are a surprising number of knife grinders around the world that still practice this trade. Here are a few modern photos taken in Paris, by a local named Francis, in the 11th arrondissement. He is one of six *le rémouleurs* that still practices in Paris. On the edge of the man's cart, you can see drawings of a pair of scissors, a knife, and what might possibly be a cleaver.

One of the last *arrotinos* in Rome, named Carmine Mainella, was interviewed in 2013 by a journalist with the *New York Times* in an article called "Rescuing City's Aging Blades, a Member of a Dying Trade." Mainella has been practicing for several decades, first learning as an apprentice when he was a teen. At age seventy-five at the time of his interview, the entire city knows him.

Though he's seen a decline in his services over the years due to the "buy new" mentality of modern times, he has been able to support himself, and his family for his whole life. He is quite possibly one of the last arrotinos in Rome. When talking about eventually retiring from his trade, Mainella said:

> *"I am sorry that one day I will have to leave it. But like everyone, sooner or later we all have to leave everything."*

That is the way of life, isn't it?

Orgy Planner

Requirements: Attention to detail, taste for debauchery

Job Status: Active

Let's end this chapter on a climax in every way possible. In BCE times, you had to know someone who knew someone to get in touch with an orgy planner, but once you did, all your wildest desires were very near.

Despite the obvious difference, this job was kind of like being a regular party planner. They had to orchestrate the food, drink, location, participants, guest list, music, and more. Having serious attention to detail was the main requirement, because often these revelries went on for *days*.

There was dancing, copulating, sometimes killing (mania is a real thing), singing, and general merrymaking. Once, the Emperor Claudius' wife, Messalina, got so carried away that she married someone else at the festivities. She quickly got her head chopped off. One party got so wild, that they took to the streets of Athens, chopping off the stone phalluses of the Hermes statues that often decorated the front of people's residences, a symbolic sculpture to bring luck and fertility.

The orgies of this time were nothing quite like the amateur orgies of today—not like I would know what the orgies of today are like. Being an orgy orchestrator was a lot of hard work, and an important job. Orgies were important social events in Greek and Roman society. Aside from the indulgent pleasure of it all, how over-the-top your orgy was said a great deal about your status. Once the fun was over, however, orgy planners were mostly outcasts from polite society. Those in lower classes were angered at the extravagant expense (and probably kind of pissed at not being invited!).

Now, I'm just *guessing* this occupation is still active. Orgies still happen nowadays, so, it's only sensible to assume *someone* organizes them. Not that I would know personally that they still happen.

CLOSING THE
CREAKY CABINET

We are coming to the end of the shelf in the cabinet of our curious history. At least, the end of *one* shelf. There is so much more to explore in our past. So many more opportunities to incredulously ask, "We did that?" I hope this book has sparked a curiosity in you to continue opening the metaphorical cabinet, to continue seeking and smiling at all the interesting things we've done, said, and believed in through the ages.

Since books can only contain so much information between their covers (and authors have only so much time to research and write—I have orgies to attend), in this book we've only scratched the surface of our lottery ticket to amusement. Hopefully, if this sells more than ten copies (all bought by my mom), then there will be more books like this to come. If not, there is a beautiful invention called the internet that has the answers for you. Also, the library. By the way, who "invented" the library? That will be your first task.

If there is anything I've learned along this journey, and I hope you did too, it is how we are both brilliant, and fallible. Our species has thought up the most fascinating solutions to problems we didn't know we had. We've made embarrassing errors, because we're as flawed as the next person. We believe in the weirdest things, just because, why not? So, dear reader, let's not judge our ancestors too harshly. After all, in a few hundred years, *we* will be the crazy ancestors who look like we didn't know what the hell we were doing. And the cycle will repeat! Here is to our future brilliance, the lack thereof, and undeniable ingenuity.

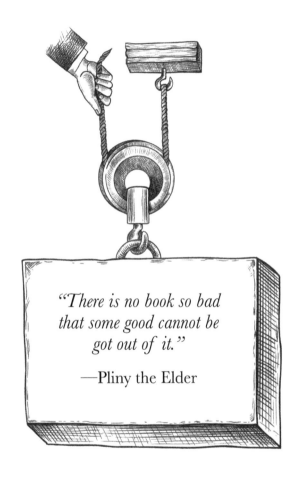

"*There is no book so bad that some good cannot be got out of it.*"

—Pliny the Elder

REFERENCES

We Did That? Bloopers, Blunders, and the Bizarre

Abbott, Geoffrey. *The Executioner Always Chops Twice: Ghastly Blunders on the Scaffold.* New York: St. Martin's Press, 2002.

Anderson, Cass. "Modern Day Gladiator Defends His 'Shin Kicking Championship' World Title And This Sport Looks F'n Incredible." BroBible. July 2019. https://brobible.com/sports/article/shin-kicking-championship-recap/.

Andrews, Stefan. "The Thai Queen who Drowned Because an Ancient Law Forbade Touching a Royal." Vintage News. April 30, 2018. https://www.thevintagenews.com/2018/04/30/thai-queen/.

Avakian, Talia. "16 odd things that are illegal in Singapore." Business Insider. August 4, 2015. https://www.businessinsider.com/things-that-are-illegal-in-singapore-2015-7.

Bill, Bryan. "Hy-Brasil: The Legendary Phantom Island of Ireland." Ancient Origins. March 12, 2019. https://www.ancient-origins.net/unexplained-phenomena/hy-brasil-legendary-phantom-island-ireland-003608.

Blome, Richard. *A New Mapp of America Septentrionale*, 1693. Courtesy of The Glen McLaughlin Map Collection of California as an Island.

Bouton, Terynn. "Mozart's Much Less Family Friendly Works" Today I Found Out. May 20, 2014. http://www.todayifoundout.com/index.php/2014/05/mozart-wrote-song-called-lick-arse-right-well-clean/.

Boyer, Crispin. *Famous Fails*. National Geographic, Washington, DC.

Broome, Fiona. "Hy-Brasil: The Other Atlantis of Irish Legend." Historic Mysteries. December 31, 2010. https://www.historicmysteries.com/hy-brasil-the-other-atlantis/.

Brueghel, Peiter. *Peasant Wedding Dance*, c. 1607. Courtesy of the Walter Arts Museum. Acquired by Henry Walters.

Cavendish, Richard. "Siam Becomes Thailand." History Today. June 23, 2014. https://www.historytoday.com/archive/siam-becomes-thailand.

Charney, Noah. "The Ghent Altarpiece: the truth about the most stolen artwork of all time." *The Guardian*. December 20, 2013.

Clare, Sean. "Illegal mince pies and other UK legal legends." BCC News. April 6, 2012. https://www.bbc.com/news/magazine-17610820.

Cockburn, Harry. "The UK's strangest laws that are still enforced." *The Independent*. September 8, 2016. https://www.independent.co.uk/news/uk/home-news/uk-strangest-weird-laws-enforced-christopher-sargeant-sturgeon-armour-a7232586.html.

Dearlove, Jack. "How the Sinking of the Titanic Was Reported." Journalism.co.uk. April 13, 2012.

Dvosky, George. "The Most Inaccurate Headline in the History of the Universe." iO9. October 29, 2013.

Faber, Toby. "A Legendary Publishing House's Most Infamous Rejection Letters." Literary Hub. September 12, 2019. https://lithub.com/a-legendary-publishing-houses-most-infamous-rejection-letters/.

Gebco. "'Disappearance of Sandy Island.'" December 2012. https://www.gebco.net/news_and_media/gebco_and_sandy_island.html.

Geologic Face on Mars Formation. 1976. NASA ID: PIA01141. Courtesy of NASA. Public Domain.

Gibson, Nathan. "Typos That Had Huge Unexpected Consequences." Ranker.

Gosline, Sheldon Lee. "'I am a fool': Dr. Henry Cattell's Private Confession about What Happened to Whitman's Brain." *Walt Whitman Quarterly Review* Vol. 3 No. 4.

Hannah Dagoe resisting execution. C. 18th century. Newgate Calendar.

Henderson, Corey; Rollman, Dan. *The Recordsetter Book of World Records.* Workman Publishing, 2011.

History.info. "1615: Turkish Sultan who Liked Bigger Women." May 2011.

Klevantseva, Tatiana. "Prominent Russians: Fyodor I "The Bellringer." Russiapedia. https://russiapedia.rt.com/prominent-russians/history-and-mythology/fyodor-i-the-bellringer/.

Kompster, "The Ten Rules of Shin-Kicking." https://www.kompster.com/featured/ten-rules-shin-kicking.

Kruse, Colton. "The Dancing Plague: Choreomania," *Ripley's Believe It or Not.* July 11, 2016. https://www.ripleys.com/weird-news/dancing-plague-choreomania/.

Lee, Sidney. *Shakespeare's Handwriting.* London: Smith, Elder and Co., 1899.

Library of Congress, Prints & Photographs Division, photograph by Harris & Ewing, Reproduction number LC-DIG-hec-31631.

Long, Tony. "July 22, 1962: Mariner 1 Done in by a Typo." WIRED. July 22, 2009.

Mabillard, Amanda. "Playing Fast and Loose with Shakespeare's Name." Shakespeare Online. 20 July. 2011. http://www.shakespeare-online.com/biography/shakespearename.html >.

Maxwell, Rebecca. "The Map Myth of Sandy Island." GisLounge. May 9, 2012. https://www.gislounge.com/the-map-myth-of-sandy-island/.

Maylan, Greg. "The Mystery of an Island That Isn't There." Auckland Museum. November 23, 2012. https://www.aucklandmuseum.com/2012/11/the-mystery-of-an-island-that-isnt-there.

McAlister, Neil Harding. *The Dancing Pilgrims at Muelebeek*, *Journal of the History of Medicine and Allied Sciences*, Volume XXXII, Issue 3, July 1977, Pages 315–319, https://doi.org/10.1093/jhmas/XXXII.3.315.

Medrano, Kastalia. "The Weirdest Laws in All 50 States." Thrillist. https://www.thrillist.com/entertainment/nation/weird-state-laws.

Mikkelson, David. "Dord: The Word That Didn't Exist." Snopes. January 4, 2015.

Mother Nature Network. https://www.mnn.com/earth-matters/animals/stories/21-animals-with-completely-ridiculous-names.

National Park Service. "Thomas Edison." https://www.nps.gov/edis/learn/historyculture/edison-biography.htm.

Oakley, Nicola. "Owning one pet goldfish is illegal in Switzerland—and the reason might make you feel guilty." Mirror. July 28, 2016. https://www.mirror.co.uk/news/weird-news/owning-one-pet-goldfish-illegal-8511105.

Redd, Wyatt. "Fart Proudly: Ben Franklin Loved Farting So Much He Wrote An Essay About It." All That's Interesting. December 8, 2017. https://allthatsinteresting.com/ben-franklin-fart-proudly.

Ridgway, Claire. "The Downfall of Margaret Pole, Countess of Salisbury, by Alexander Taylor." Tudor Society. 2015. https://www.tudorsociety.com/the-downfall-of-margaret-pole-countess-of-salisbury-by-alexander-taylor/.

Ridgway, Claire. "The Execution of Margaret Pole, Countess of Salisbury." The Anne Boleyn Files. May 27, 2010. https://www.theanneboleynfiles.com/the-execution-of-margaret-pole-countess-of-salisbury/.

Rigg, Jamie. "Fiske's Reading Machine was a Pre-Silicon Kindle." Engadget. July 6, 2018.

Robinson, Melia; Sterbenz, Christina; and Martin, Emmie. "The 17 strangest laws in America." Business Insider. March 6, 2015. https://www.businessinsider.com/strangest-most-ridiculous-laws-in-america-2015-3.

Sanson, Nicolas. *Americqve Septentrionale*, c. 1682. Courtesy of The Glen McLaughlin Map Collection of California as an Island.

Singh KC, Sanjaya. "Thaneswar Guragai of Nepal breaks 14 Guinness World Record titles and still counting!" BlankPage. February 20, 2017. https://sanjayakc.wordpress.com/2017/02/20/thaneswar-guragai-of-nepal-breaks-14-guinness-world-records-and-still-counting/.

Spencer Collection, The New York Public Library. "Horae," New York Public Library Digital Collections. http://digitalcollections. nypl.org/items/1205b8f0-e35f-0135-3c6d-771f88f25699.

Sports Weird-O-Pedia: The Ultimate Book of Surprising, Strange, and Incredibly Bizarre Facts About Sports. Freedman, Lew. New York: Racehorse Publishing, 2019.

Sterbenz, Christina. "The Entire 'Popeye' Franchise Is Based On Bad Science." *Business Insider.* January 17, 2014. https://www. businessinsider.com/spinach-typo-popeye-2014-1.

The Huffington Post. "Titanic Headlines In Vancouver Got It Very Wrong." October 30, 2013.

The New York Times. "Woolen Mill Co-Owner Dies After Being Wrapped in Yarn." August 12, 1987.

The Saint Paul Globe. (St. Paul, Minn.), 30 April 1905. Chronicling America: Historic American Newspapers. Lib. of Congress. <https://chroniclingamerica.loc.gov/lccn/sn90059523/1905-04-30/ed-1/seq-12/>.

The Salt Lake Tribune. "Mars Peopled by One Vast Thinking Vegetable." October 13, 1912.

Trista. "The Young Queen Sunandha Died From Drowning Because the Law Forbade Anybody to Touch Her By Pain of Death." History Collection. https://historycollection.co/the-young-queen-sunandha-died-from-drowning-because-the-law-forbade-anybody-to-touch-her-by-pain-of-death/.

Usher, Shaun. "Oh my ass burns like fire!" Letters of Note. July 5, 2012. http://www.lettersofnote.com/2012/07/oh-my-ass-burns-like-fire.html.

van Eyck, Jan. *Het Lam Gods* (middenstuk),1430–1432. Sint-Baafskathedraal te Gent. Saint-Bavo's cathedral Ghent.

Vellut, Guilhem. "Naki Sumo Baby Crying Contest." *Atlas Obscura.*

Vinckeboons, Joan. *Map of California shown as an island.* Public Domain. LCCN: 99443375. Call info: G3291.S12 coll .H3.

Vízkelety Béla Eger vár ostroma. c. 1890. Courtesy of Bródy Sándor Könyvatar Libarary.

Winters, S. R. "Stretching the Five-Foot Shelf." *Scientific American,* 1922.

Wood, Jennifer. "10 Rejection Letters Sent to Very Successful People." Mental Floss. March 5, 2014. http://mentalfloss.com/article/55416/10-rejection-letters-sent-famous-people.

We Believed That? Superstitions

"Gaspar Schott." Wikipedia. June 02, 2018. Accessed 2019. https://en.wikipedia.org/wiki/Gaspar_Schott.

"Monsters and Monstrosities: The Marvels and Wonders of the 'Physica Curiosa,' 1662." DangerousMinds. April 04, 2017. Accessed March 07, 2019. https://dangerousminds.net/comments/monsters_and_monstrosities_the_marvels_and_wonders_of_the_physica_curiosa_1.

"The Scientific American Supplement. Index for Vol.62." 1906. Scientific American 62 (1617supp): 25915–16. https://doi.org/10.1038/scientificamerican12291906-25915supp.

Baxamusa, Batul Nafisa. 2018. "Orchid Flower Meaning and Symbolism: A Really Interesting Read." Gardenerdy. January 29, 2018. https://gardenerdy.com/orchid-flower-meaning.

Bergen, Fanny D., and William Wells Newell. 2007. Current Superstitions: Collected from the Oral Tradition of English Speaking Folk. Teddington, Middlesex: Echo Library.

Bowman, Ben. 2017. "The Origin of Throwing Rice At Weddings." Curiosity.com. August 2017. https://curiosity.com/topics/the-origin-of-throwing-rice-at-weddings/.

British Archaeological Association. 1895. *The Journal of the British Archaeological Association*. Vol. 1. Henry G. Bohn. 1 January 1895.

Cielo, Astra. *Signs, Omens and Superstitions*. New York: George Sully and Company, 1918.

Costantino, Grace. "Five 'Real' Sea Monsters Brought to Life by Early Naturalists." Smithsonian.com. October 27, 2014. https://www.smithsonianmag.com/science-nature/five-real-sea-monsters-brought-life-early-naturalists-180953155/?page=1.

CRRC. "The Orchid in the Human Imagination." n.d. Center for Research in Reproduction and Contraception. Accessed April 26, 2019. http://depts.washington.edu/popctr/orchids.htm.

Cryer, Max. 2016. *Superstitions and Why We Have Them*. Strawberry Hills, NSW: ReadHowYouWant.

Cuming, Henry Syer. "Shoe Lore." In *Journal of the British Archaeological Association*, edited by British Archaeological Association, 148—153. London: Bedford Press, 1895.

Czartoryski, Alex. 2011. "Lost At Sea: 5 Stories of Disappearing Ships." Boating Safety and Safe Boating Blog. March 2011. https://www.boaterexam.com/blog/2011/03/lost-at-sea.aspx.

Daniels, Cora Linn, and C. M. Stevens. 2003. *Encyclopædia of Superstitions, Folklore, and the Occult Sciences of the World: a Comprehensive*

Library of Human Belief and Practice in the Mysteries of Life. 1903.
Honolulu: University Press of the Pacific.

Erbland, Kate. 2014. "7 Tooth Fairy Traditions from Around the
World." Mental Floss. August 22, 2014. http://mentalfloss.com/
article/58503/7-tooth-fairy-traditions-around-world.

Fitzgerald, James. *The Joys of Smoking Cigarettes.* New York:
HarperCollins, 2007.

Grammarist. "If the Shoe Fits and If the Cap Fits." n.d. Accessed
April 17, 2019. https://grammarist.com/idiom/if-the-shoe-fits-
and-if-the-cap-fits/.

Heit, Judi. "Schooner Patriot and the Mystery of Theodosia
Burr Alston—January 1813." January 01, 1970. http://
northcarolinashipwrecks.blogspot.com/2012/04/schooner-patriot-
and-mystery-of.html.

Hibbert, Christopher, and David Starkey. 2007. *Charles I: A Life of
Religion, War and Treason.* Basingstoke: Palgrave Macmillan.

Hingston, Michael. 2014. "Don't Tell the Kids: The Real History
of the Tooth Fairy." Salon. February 8, 2014. https://www.salon.
com/2014/02/09/dont_tell_the_kids_the_real_history_of_the_
tooth_fairy/.

Houlbrook, Dr. Ceri. *The Concealed Revealed.* "The Folklore of Shoe-
Shaped Confetti." July 28, 2016. https://theconcealedrevealed.
wordpress.com/2016/07/28/the-folklore-of-shoe-shaped-confetti/.

Kanner, Leo, 1894–1981. *Folklore of the Teeth.* New York: The
Macmillan company, 1928.

Lys, Claudia de. *What's So Lucky about a Four-Leaf Clover? And 8414 Other
Strange and Fascinating Superstitions from around the World.* New York:
Bell Publishing Company, 1989.

Matsuo, Alex. *The Haunted Actor: An Exploration of Supernatural Belief through Theatre*. Bloomington: AuthorHouse, 2014.

Mikkelson, David. "Fact Check: 'Bananas on a Boat' Superstition." Snopes.com. November 2012. Accessed 2019. https://www.snopes.com/fact-check/banana-ban/.

Murrell, Deborah. 2008. *Superstitions: 1,013 of the Wackiest Myths, Fables & Old Wives Tales*. Pleasantville, NY: Readers Digest.

Opie, Iona Archibald and Peter Opie. *The Lore and Language of Schoolchildren*. New York: New York Review Books, 2001. https://books.google.com/books?id=ZDUSAAAAYAAJ&printsec=frontcover&source=gbs_ge_summary_r&cad=0#v=onepage&q&f=false (Wedding Superstitions 7-16).

Opie, Iona Archibald, and Peter Opie. 2001. *The Lore and Language of Schoolchildren*. New York: New York Review Books.

Phrases.org. "Bad Luck Comes in Threes—Phrase Meaning and Origin." Accessed May 2, 2019. https://www.phrases.org.uk/bulletin_board/32/messages/643.html.

Pickering, David. *Cassell Dictionary of Superstitions*. London: Cassell, 1995.

Punch, or *The London Charivari* magazine, March 11, 1854, vol. 26, p. 100. Punch cartoon, 1854, depicting Queen Victoria 'Throwing the Old Shoe' after her soldiers as they depart for the Crimean War.

Rachel's English. "10 Everyday Idioms." January 2019. https://www.youtube.com/watch?v=cnFdm8_nArQ.

Ringmar. "Politics without Borders: The Royal Touch." History of International Relations. http://ringmar.net/

politicaltheoryfornomads/index.php/category/an-anarchist-history-of-the-state/sources/.

Sacred Texts. n.d. "Throwing the Shoe." The Origins of Popular Superstitions and Customs: Marriage Superstitions and Customs: (6) Throwing The Shoe. Accessed 2019. http://www.sacred-texts.com/neu/eng/osc/osc38.htm.

Strom, Caleb. 2018. "Tooth Fairy Tales: The Strange Origins of the Dental Sprite." Ancient Origins. August 10, 2018. https://www.ancient-origins.net/myths-legends-europe/tooth-fairy-0010523.

Tolliver, Lee. 2012. "Old Fishermen's Tales: The Curse of the Banana." Pilot. July 23, 2012. https://pilotonline.com/sports/outdoors/article_3b4ecc9f-1753-5e30-b5d5-08fabed0d734.html.

Webster, Richard. *The Encyclopedia of Superstitions*. Woodbury: Llewellyn Publications, 2008.

Webster, Richard. *The Encyclopedia of Superstitions*. Woodbury: Llewellyn Publications, 2008.

Wenegenofsky, Joe. 1996. "The Forbidden Fruit." TheFisherman.com. 1996. https://www.thefisherman.com/index.cfm?fuseaction=feature.display&feature_ID=827&ParentCat=2.

Willis, Richard. *USS Wasp*. https://flic.kr/p/cYiKNs. (Photo only.)

Writing Explained. "What Does Shoe Is On the Other Foot Mean?" n.d. Writing Explained. Accessed 2019. https://writingexplained.org/idiom-dictionary/shoe-is-on-the-other-foot.

We Prescribed That? Medical Cures, Quacks, and Craziness

A crowd of spectators wait as Tom Idle is driven in a cart with his coffin to his place of execution and the gallows. Engraving by William Hogarth, 1747. Credit: Wellcome Collection. Creative Commons.

A early blood transfusion from lamb to man. Credit: Wellcome Collection. Creative Commons.

Ausschnitt. Von dem allerbesten Land so auff Erden ligt. 1671. Public Domain.

Barbara's Banter. "Bon Appétit." August 24, 2014. http://www. barbdahlgren.com/?p=2359.

Barrett, Erin; Mingo, Jack. *Doctors Killed George Washington.* Conari Press.

Bermudez, Esmeralda. "'Vivaporu': For many Latinos, memories of Vicks VapoRub are as strong as the scent of eucalyptus." *Los Angeles Times.* March 26, 2019.

Charleston, Libby-Jane. "Chastity Belts and Crocodile Dung: A History of Birth Control." *HuffPost.* December 30, 2016.

Darby, Marta. "El Bix—A Cuban Cure for All That Ails You." My Big Fat Cuban Family. March 8, 2011.

Davis, Matt. "19th-century medicine: Milk was used as a blood substitute for transfusions." Big Think. April 17, 2019.

Dolan, Maria. "The Gruesome History of Eating Corpses As Medicine." *Smithsonian Magazine.* May 6, 2012.

Forth, Christopher. "The Lucrative Black Market in Human Fat." *The Atlantic.* May 26, 2019.

Goldstein, Darra. "A Medieval Russian Hangover Cure." https:// recipes.hypotheses.org/3979.

Griffith, Ivor; editor. *American Journal of Pharmacy and the Sciences Supporting Public Health*, Volume 94. Philadelphia College of Pharmacy and Science. P. 665–671. 1922.

Kang, Lydia, MD; Pedersen, Nate. *Quackery: A Brief History of the Worst Ways to Cure Everything*. Workman Publishing 2017, New York.

Kelsey-Sugg, Anna. "The laughing gas parties of the 1700s—and how they sparked a medical breakthrough." ABC National Radio. February 20, 2019.

Krichbaum, J. G. US Patent Office. US268693. December 5, 1882.

Ricotti, Eugenia Salza Prina. *Meals and Recipes from Ancient Greece*. Getty Publications 2007.

Robert Seymour, 1829, etching. Public Domain. Almapatter44.

Rodriguez Mcrobbie, Linda. "9 Fascinating Historic Methods of Contraception." Mental Floss. February 25, 2013

Smith, Lesley. The Kahun Gynaecological Papyrus: ancient Egyptian medicine. BMJ Sexual & Reproductive Health.

Stephen, Leslie; Lee, Sir Sidney. *Dictionary of National Biography*. Smith, Elder, & Company, 1890.

Sugg, Richard. "Corpse medicine: mummies, cannibals, and vampires." *The Lancet.* June 21, 2008.

Sugg, Richard. *Mummies, Cannibals, and Vampires: The History of Corpse Medicine from the Renaissance to the Victorians*. Routledge 2011.

The brains of dissected heads. Photolithograph, 1940, after a woodcut, 1543. Credit: Wellcome Collection. Creative Commons.

the Elder, Pliny. *The Natural History of Pliny*, volume 4 (of 6).

Vester, Franz. US Patent Office. US81437. August 25, 1868.

We Invented That? Surprising and Wacky Inventions

Amphibious Bike / Cyclomer. Flickr Commons. Nationaal Archief / Spaarnestad Photo / Fotograaf onbekend, SFA002005344. https://www.flickr.com/photos/nationaalarchief/4193508602/.

Art and Picture Collection, The New York Public Library. "Sunshade For Vehicles." New York Public Library Digital Collections. http://digitalcollections.nypl.org/items/510d47e1-3383-a3d9-e040-e00a18064a99. (The Early Visor photo and reference.)

Battle, Daniel S. "Flood protection container for vehicles." US Patent Office; US4315535.

Bertolini Giuseppe (Us). Ocean Floating Safe. United States. Menotti Nanni. US1166145. http://www.freepatentsonline.com/1166145.html (The Unsinkable Safe photo and reference.)

BM Reims, Public Domain, https://commons.wikimedia.org/w/index.php?curid=48571590.

Fawcett, Bill. *It Looked Good on Paper: Bizarre Inventions, Design Disasters, and Engineering Follies.* New York: Harper Collins, 2009.

Folsom, Dwane. Canine Scuba Diving Apparatus. US Patent 6,206,00 B1. March 27, 2001.

George Arents Collection, The New York Public Library. "X-ray apparatus." New York Public Library Digital Collections. Accessed January 28, 2019. http://digitalcollections.nypl.org/items/510d47e2-4734-a3d9-e040-e00a18064a99. (Chapter cover photo.)

Hedley, Ralph (died 1913)—BBC Your Paintings (now available by Art UK), Public Domain, https://commons.wikimedia.org/w/index.php?curid=27892392.

In70mm. "Behind the Scenes of 'Scent of Mystery' in Glorious Smell-O-Vision." YouTube. December 04, 2015. https://www.youtube.com/watch?v=mRdEbb3_YEE.

Laube, Carmen. "A Brief History about Hans Laube: A Personal Reflection on the Osmologist Responsible for Smell-O-Vision." *In 70 mm*. https://www.in70mm.com/news/2016/hans_laube/index.htm.

National Archives Catalog. National Archives ID 45499786. Local ID 165-WW-272D-3. Photographer: Underwood and Underwood. https://catalog.archives.gov/id/45499786. (Unsinkable safe photos and reference.)

Pollack, Rich. "Beyond 'Sit,' 'Speak' and 'Stay': Shadow, the Scuba-Diving Dog." *Orlando Sentinel*. October 25, 1993. https://www.orlandosentinel.com/news/os-xpm-1993-10-25-9310250320-story.html.

Seymour, Robert. Two men wearing revolving top hats with several attachments for optical aids and tobacco etc. Colored etching by R. Seymour, 1830. Courtesy of Wellcome Library.

VanCleave, Ted. *Totally Absurd Inventions*. Andrews McMeel, Kansas City. 2001.

Williams, James A. Animal-Trap. Specification forming part of Letters Patent No. 269,766. Dated December 26, 1882. (The Mousetrap Pistol photo and reference.)

We Did That? Pain (and Death) Is Beauty

Addison, Joseph. *The Spectator,* "Party Patches." June 2, 1711. http://www.aboutenglish.it/englishpress/spectator81.htm.

Arsenic Complexion Wafers. *The Cosmopolitan Magazine*, Feb 1896. Flickr. https://flic.kr/p/ou5B9P.

Art and Picture Collection, The New York Public Library. "Poulaine Avec Chainettes." New York Public Library Digital Collections. Accessed August 29, 2019. http://digitalcollections.nypl.org/items/510d47e1-3274-a3d9-e040-e00a18064a99.

Banner, Lois W. *American Beauty*. New York: Knopf, 1983.

Bowman, Karen. *Corsets and Codpieces: A History of Outrageous Fashion, from Roman Times to the Modern Era*. Skyhorse Publishing, 2016.

Collectors Weekly. May 4, 2017. https://www.collectorsweekly.com/articles/sexy-face-stickers/.

Cosgrave, Bronwyn. The Complete History of Costume and Fashion: From Ancient Egypt to the Present Day. New York: Checkmark Books, 2000. http://www.fashionencyclopedia.com/fashion_costume_culture/Early-Cultures-Europe-in-the-Middle-Ages/Crackowes-and-Poulaines.html#ixzz5y0PkdsDu.

Detail of a 15th century illuminated manuscript of Renaud de Montaubon. Public Domain.

Diary of Samuel Pepys. September 26, 1664. https://www.pepysdiary.com/diary/1664/09/.

Dieulefils, Pierre. *La Rieuse Aux Dents Noires* (Black-Toothed Laughter). Tonkin woman with blackened teeth. Public Domain. http://nguyentl.free.fr/autrefois/scenes/peuple/tonkin_femme1.jpg.

Docevski, Boban. "In 1929, Spruce Veneer Bathing Suits Were Described as Simple, Cheap, and Easy to Make, Yet Fashionable and Modern." *The Vintage News*. September 26, 2016. https://www.thevintagenews.com/2016/09/26/priority-spruce-girls-ladies-wearing-spruce-veneer-bathing-suits-1929-2/.

Eldridge, Lisa. *Face Paint: The Story of Makeup*. New York: Abrams Image, 2015.

Gilbert, Rosalie. "Medieval Women's Hats and Hennins." Rosalie's Medieval Woman. www.rosaliegilbert.com/hatsandhennins.html.

Gilles Edme Petit. *Le Matin*. Public Domain. Courtesy of the Metropolitan Museum of Art. Accession Number: 53.600.1042. https://www.metmuseum.org/art/collection/search/388453.

Herman, Eleanor. *The Royal Art of Poison: Filthy Palaces, Fatal Cosmetics, Deadly Medicine, and Murder Most Foul*. New York: St. Martin's Press, 2018.

Hernandez, Rigoberto. "Wonderful, Ridiculous, Head-Scratchingly Pointy Mexican Boots Are Now A Designer Item." National Public Radio. March 26, 2015. https://www.npr.org/sections/codeswitch/2015/03/26/395391623/wonderful-ridiculous-head-scratchingly-pointy-mexican-boots-are-now-a-designer-i.

Hyland, Veronique. "Yes, Men in the 18th Century Wore Corsets." The Cut. April 6, 2015.

Imbler, Sabrina. "Why Were Medieval Europeans So Obsessed With Long, Pointy Shoes?" *Atlas Obscura*. May 22, 2019. https://www.atlasobscura.com/articles/medieval-europeans-pointy-shoes.

Kunisada, Utagawa. Woodblock print by Kunisada I, signed "Gototei Kunisada ga," series: Mirrors of the Modern Boudoir, title *Tooth Blackening*, published by Azumaya Daisuke, c. 1823. File derived

from Public Domain, https://commons.wikimedia.org/w/index.
php?curid=66250607.

Little, Becky. 2016. "Arsenic Pills and Lead Foundation: The History
of Toxic Makeup." *National Geographic.* National Geographic
Society. September 22, 2016. https://news.nationalgeographic.
com/2016/09/ingredients-lipstick-makeup-cosmetics-
science-history/.

Lubitz, Rachel. 2019. "Nail Polish for Men Is Finally 'Normal'—Just
Like It Used to Be 5,000 Years Ago." Mic. May 7, 2019. https://
www.mic.com/articles/136830/nail-polish-for-men-is-finally-
normal-just-like-it-used-to-be-5-000-years-ago.

Mallory, Aileen. 1995. "Don't Know Much About History."
NAILS Magazine. January 1, 1995. https://www.nailsmag.com/
article/40736/dont-know-much-about-history.

Miller, Harry L. US Patent Office, 1901. US667447A.

Montaigne, Marie. *How to Be Beautiful.* New York: Harper, 1913.

Montealegre, Hazel Mann. US Patent Office, 1924. US1497342A.

Oatman-Sanford, Hunter. "That Time the French Aristocracy Was
Obsessed With Sexy Face Stickers."

Oliveras, Chloe. 2012. "The Colorful History of Nail Polish." The
Independent Florida Alligator. April 25, 2012. https://www.
alligator.org/blogs/lifestyle/thefbomb/article_92924820-8e3d-
11e1-b5bf-001a4bcf887a.html.

Rance, Caroline. 2018. "Dr MacKenzie's Improved Harmless
Arsenic Complexion Wafers." The Quack Doctor. October 9,
2018. http://thequackdoctor.com/index.php/dr-mackenzies-
improved-harmless-arsenic-complexion-wafers/.

Riordan, Teresa. *Inventing Beauty: A History of the Innovations that Have Made Us Beautiful.* New York: Broadway Books, 2004.

Sears, Roebuck & Co. Catalogue 1897. P.31. Editor Fred L. Israel. Chelsea House Publishers, NY. 1968. https://hdl.handle.net/2027/uc1.31158001963940.

Sun, Feifei. "These Boots Were Made for Dancing: Pointy Shoes South of the Border," *TIME.* March 27, 2012. https://time.com/3787277/pointy-shoes/.

University of Virginia. "Reshaping the Body: Men's Corsets."

Utamaro, Kitagawa. *Yamauba Blackening Her Teeth and Kintoki.* 1795. Courtesy of The Metropolitan Museum of Art (public domain). Accession No. 1996.463.

van der Weyden, Rogier. *Portrait of a Lady.* C. 1460. National Gallery of Art. Andrew W. Mellon Collection.

Wooden Bathing Suit. Nationaal Archief / Spaarnestad Photo / Fotograaf onbekend, SFA002009921. https://www.flickr.com/photos/nationaalarchief/4194412077/. (Photo only.)

We Did That? Odd Jobs

"Augury." Occtulopedia. http://www.occultopedia.com/a/augury.htm.

"Extispicy." Occtulopedia. http://www.occultopedia.com/e/extispicy.htm.

"Haruspex." World Wide Words. http://www.worldwidewords.org/weirdwords/ww-har1.htm.

Adriaen van Ostade. *The Knife Grinder / Le Rémouleur.* Holland, Haarlem, 1610–1685. Courtesy of the Los Angeles County Museum of Art.

Bartsch, Adam von. *The Illustrated Bartsch*. New York: Abaris Books, 1978.

Bilger, Burkhard. "The Eternal Seductive Beauty of Feathers." *The New Yorker*. September 18, 2017.

Bruce, Andrea. "Finding Dignity in a Dirty Job," *National Geographic*. April, 2019 Issue.

Dhwty. "Ancient Roman Curse Tablets Invoke Goddess Sulis Minerva to Kill and Maim." Ancient Origins. April 14, 2015. https://www.ancient-origins.net/artifacts-other-artifacts/ancient-roman-curse-tablets-invoke-goddess-sulis-minerva-020296.

Erenow. "The Night-Soil Men." August 28, 2019. https://erenow.net/modern/the-ghost-map/2.php.

Francis. *Knife Grinder*. May 19, 2008. https://commons.wikimedia.org/wiki/File:Knife_grinder-1.JPG.

Griffiths, Sarah. " 'May the thief go mad and blind!': Roman 'curse tablets' etched with messages of revenge are added to the heritage register." *Daily Mail*. June 25, 2014. https://www.dailymail.co.uk/sciencetech/article-2669296/May-thief-mad-blind-Roman-curse-tablets-etched-messages-revenge-added-heritage-register.html.

History Undusted. "Knockers Up." Photos only. https://historyundusted.wordpress.com/tag/knocker-up/.

Hollstein, F. W. H. Dutch and Flemish Etchings, Engravings, and Woodcuts, ca. 1450-1700. Amsterdam: M. Hertzberger, 1949. https://www.atlasobscura.com/articles/when-american-cities-were-full-of-crap.

Kelley, Debra. 2016. "10 Crazy Tales Of History's Food Tasters." Listverse. May 23, 2016. https://listverse.com/2016/05/23/10-

tales-of-sacrifice-and-ceremony-about-historys-hidden-food-tasters/.

Leon, Vicki. W*orking IX to V: Orgy Planners, Funeral Clowns, and Other Prized Professions of the Ancient World*. Walker Books: New York, 2007.

Leon, Vicki. *Working IX to V: Orgy Planners, Funeral Clowns, and Other Prized Professions of the Ancient World*. Walker Books: New York, 2007.

Luthern, Ashley. 2009. "Testing for Poison Still a Profession for Some." Smithsonian.com. Smithsonian Institution. June 26, 2009. https://www.smithsonianmag.com/arts-culture/testing-for-poison-still-a-profession-for-some-61805292/.

Mark, Joshua J. 2019. "Vestal Virgin." Ancient History Encyclopedia. Ancient History Encyclopedia. July 2, 2019. https://www.ancient.eu/Vestal_Virgin/.

Menkes, Suzy. "Andre Lemarie Is the Last of the Plumassier Breed : A King of Haute Couture Feathers Reigns Supreme." *The New York Times*. December 15, 1998.

Mingren, Wu. n.d. "A Deadly Bite: The Plight of the Ancient Food Taster." Ancient Origins. Ancient Origins. Accessed August 13, 2019. https://www.ancient-origins.net/history-famous-people/deadly-bite-plight-ancient-food-taster-009193.

Moon, Jay. "The Industrial Revolution's Peashooting Human Alarm Clocks." INISH. April 22, 2016. https://insh.world/history/the-industrial-revolutions-peashooting-human-alarm-clocks/.

Patchett, Merle. "The Last Plumassier: Storying Dead Birds, Gender and Paraffection at Maison Lemarié." Sage Publishing, *Cultural Geographies*, 2018, Vol. 25(1) 123–134.

Peek, Sitala. "Knocker uppers: Waking up the workers in industrial Britain." BBC News. March 27, 2016. https://www.bbc.com/news/uk-england-35840393.

Povoledo, Elisabetta. "Rescuing City's Aging Blades, a Member of a Dying Trade." *The New York Times*. October 7, 2013. https://www.nytimes.com/2013/10/08/world/europe/rescuing-citys-aging-blades-a-member-of-a-dying-trade.html.

Richerman, 18th century nightman's card. Public Domain. http://www.jasa.net.au/london/sanitation.htm.

Scala. 2018. "Vestal Virgins: Rome's Most Powerful Priestesses." Vestal Virgins: Rome's Most Powerful Priestesses. December 18, 2018. https://www.nationalgeographic.com/archaeology-and-history/magazine/2018/11-12/vestal-virgins-of-ancient-rome/.

Struck, Peter T. "Haruspex." University of Pennsylvania Dictionary. http://www.classics.upenn.edu/myth/php/tools/dictionary.php?regexp=HARUSPEX&method=standard.

The Costume of Great Britain, London, England, 1805. Science Museum, London.

The Miriam and Ira D. Wallach Division of Art, Prints and Photographs: Picture Collection, The New York Public Library. "Vestal virgins serving in the temple," New York Public Library Digital Collections. http://digitalcollections.nypl.org/items/510d47e4-5f8b-a3d9-e040-e00a18064a99.

Van Haarlem, Cornelius. *Before the Deluge*. 1615. M.Ob.1472 MNW. Courtesy of Muzeum Narodowe w Warszawie. Public Domain.

Whiting, Jim. "Gong Farmers: Their Crop Was…Crap." Nonfiction Minute. April 11, 2019. https://www.nonfictionminute.org/the-nonfiction-minute/gong-farmers-their-crop-was-crap.

ABOUT THE AUTHOR

Sophie Stirling is a scholar of history and literature, her studies encompass the folklore of various cultures. She is also a self-professed literature geek, shameless punster, and believes that sharing stories, humor, and reading about history allow us to have a deeper connection with our fellow human beings, and give us a better look into our collective future. Sophie authored *We Did That?* to share her passion for learning, and her love for this wild world we live in.

Mango Publishing, established in 2014, publishes an eclectic list of books by diverse authors—both new and established voices—on topics ranging from business, personal growth, women's empowerment, LGBTQ studies, health, and spirituality to history, popular culture, time management, decluttering, lifestyle, mental wellness, aging, and sustainable living. We were recently named 2019's #1 fastest growing independent publisher by *Publishers Weekly*. Our success is driven by our main goal, which is to publish high quality books that will entertain readers as well as make a positive difference in their lives.

Our readers are our most important resource; we value your input, suggestions, and ideas. We'd love to hear from you—after all, we are publishing books for you!

Please stay in touch with us and follow us at:

Facebook: Mango Publishing
Twitter: @MangoPublishing
Instagram: @MangoPublishing
LinkedIn: Mango Publishing
Pinterest: Mango Publishing

Sign up for our newsletter at www.mango.bz and receive a free book!

Join us on Mango's journey to reinvent publishing, one book at a time.

CPSIA information can be obtained
at www.ICGtesting.com
Printed in the USA
JSHW041913011221
20867JS00017B/17